Financial Freedom for All: A Simple Guide to Achieving financial Independence

Best for 2024 and beyond

Co Author & Editor – Sandip Das

Published by – Arojit Das

Copyright © 2024 Arojit Das All rights reserved.

No part of this publication may be copied, reproduced in any format, by any means, electronic or otherwise, without prior consent from the copyright owner and publisher of the book.

Disclaimer : provided sites and names of the platforms, is for example purpose and provide assistance to the readers this book does not sponsored by any of them, and does not support them absolutely there may other Platform who might give better service. So act on your own accord.

Table of Contents :

Introduction

1. Why Financial Independence Matters

   - The importance of financial independence for everyone

   - How this book can help you achieve it

2. Overview of Financial Independence

   - Definition and benefits

   - Common misconceptions

Chapter 1: Understanding Your Financial Situation

1. Assessing Your Current Finances

   - Evaluating income, expenses, debts, and assets

   - Creating a personal balance sheet

2. Setting a Baseline

   - Establishing your starting point

   - Tracking your progress

Chapter 2: Setting Clear Financial Goals

1. Importance of Goals

   - Why setting financial goals is crucial

2. SMART Goals

   - How to set Specific, Measurable, Achievable, Relevant, and Time-bound goals

Chapter 3: Budgeting Basics

1. Creating a Budget

   - Step-by-step guide to creating a simple budget

2. Tracking Expenses

   - Methods for tracking daily, weekly, and monthly expenses

3. Adjusting Your Budget

   - How to tweak your budget to stay on track

Chapter 4: Saving Strategies for Everyone

1. Building an Emergency Fund

   - Importance of having a safety net
   - How to build your emergency fund

2. Automatic Savings

- Setting up automatic transfers to savings accounts

3. Finding Extra Savings

- Tips for cutting expenses and finding savings in daily life

Chapter 5: Managing Debt

1. Types of Debt

- Understanding good vs. bad debt

2. Debt Repayment Strategies

- Snowball vs. avalanche methods

3. Avoiding Debt Traps

- Tips for staying out of unnecessary debt

Chapter 6: Income Enhancement

1. Multiple Income Streams

- Importance of diversifying income sources

2. Side Hustles

- Ideas and tips for starting side hustles

3. Maximizing Earnings

   - Negotiation tips for higher salaries or rates

Chapter 7: Basics of Investing

1. Why Invest?

   - Importance of investing for long-term wealth

2. Types of Investments

   - Stocks, bonds, real estate, mutual funds, and ETFs

3. Starting Small

   - How to begin investing with limited funds

Chapter 8: Long-Term Financial Planning

1. Retirement Planning

   - Importance of planning for retirement early

2. Retirement Accounts

   - Overview of 401(k)s, IRAs, and other retirement accounts

3. Legacy Planning

- Basics of estate planning and ensuring your financial legacy

Chapter 9: Financial Strategies for Specific Groups

1. Young Adults

   - Handling student loans, entry-level salaries, and first-time investing

2. Single Parents

   - Budgeting on a single income, finding financial aid, and planning for children's future

3. Freelancers and Gig Workers

   - Managing irregular income, taxes, and saving for retirement

4. Retirees or Near-Retirees

   - Maximizing retirement income, managing healthcare costs, and legacy planning

5. Minorities and Underrepresented Groups

   - Overcoming financial barriers, accessing resources, and building community wealth

Chapter 10: Tools and Resources

1. Financial Tools

- Recommended apps and software for budgeting, investing, and tracking finances

2. Books and Websites

   - Further reading and reliable online resources for financial education

3. Community Support

   - Importance of building a support network and finding financial mentors

Chapter 11: Real-Life Success Stories

1. Case Studies

   - Inspirational stories from individuals in each target group who achieved financial independence

2. Lessons Learned

   - Key takeaways and practical advice from each story

Conclusion

1. Summary of Key Principles

   - Recap the main points

2. Next Steps

- Simple steps readers can take immediately to start their journey toward financial independence

Introduction

Financial independence is a transformative goal that can dramatically improve your quality of life, reduce stress, and increase your personal freedom. It's not just about having a lot of money; it's about managing your finances wisely so you can live life on your own terms. In this introduction, we will explore why financial independence matters and how this book can help you achieve it.

Why Financial Independence Matters

1. Freedom of Choice

- Career Flexibility: Financial independence allows you to choose work that you find fulfilling, rather than being tied to a job solely for the paycheck. Whether you want to switch careers, start your own business, or take a sabbatical, having financial security gives you the freedom to make those choices.

- Lifestyle Choices: You can live where you want, travel when you want, and pursue hobbies and interests without financial constraints. Financial independence empowers you to design a lifestyle that aligns with your values and desires.

2. Reduced Stress and Anxiety

- Financial Security: One of the biggest sources of stress for many people is money. By achieving financial independence, you eliminate the constant worry about bills, debt, and unexpected expenses. This security leads to better mental health and overall well-being.

- Emergency Preparedness: Having savings and investments means you are better prepared for life's unexpected events, such as medical emergencies, job loss, or other crises. This preparedness reduces anxiety and allows you to handle unforeseen circumstances more effectively.

3. Better Quality of Life

- Time Freedom: Financial independence buys you time. You can spend more time with family and friends, pursue hobbies, volunteer, or simply relax. Time is a finite resource, and financial independence allows you to use it in ways that bring you joy and satisfaction.

- Health and Well-being: With financial independence, you can afford to invest in your health by accessing better healthcare, eating healthier, and having more time to exercise and rest. Financial stress is linked to various health issues, so eliminating it can lead to a healthier life.

4. Personal Growth and Fulfillment

- Pursuing Passions: Financial independence enables you to invest time and money in your passions and interests. Whether it's furthering your education, starting a new hobby, or traveling the world, financial freedom gives you the ability to pursue what makes you happy.

- Continuous Learning: With financial security, you have the resources to continue learning and growing. This could mean taking courses, attending workshops, or simply having the time to read and explore new ideas.

5. Legacy and Impact

- Family Security: Financial independence allows you to provide for your family, ensuring that your loved ones are taken care of. You can fund your children's education, help family members in need, and leave a financial legacy.

- Charitable Giving: Financial independence enables you to give back to your community and support causes you care about. You can donate money, time, and resources to make a positive impact on the world.

How This Book Will Help You

This book is designed to guide you through the journey to financial independence, no matter where you are starting from. We will provide practical, actionable advice tailored to different life situations, including young adults, single parents, freelancers and gig workers, retirees or near-retirees, and minorities or underrepresented groups. Here's what you can expect:

- Clear and Simple Explanations: Financial concepts can be complex, but we break them down into easy-to-understand terms.

You don't need a background in finance to grasp the principles in this book.

- Actionable Steps: Each chapter includes practical steps you can take immediately to improve your financial situation. These are real-world strategies that have been proven to work.

- Tailored Advice: We recognize that financial advice is not one-size-fits-all. This book includes specific strategies for different groups to address their unique financial challenges and opportunities.

- Inspiration and Motivation: Through real-life success stories, you will see how others have achieved financial independence. These stories will inspire and motivate you to take control of your own financial future.

- Resources and Tools: Throughout the book, you will find recommendations for tools, apps, books, and other resources to help you on your journey to financial independence.

By the end of this book, you will have a solid understanding of what it takes to achieve financial independence and the steps you need to take to get there. Remember, financial independence is a journey, not a destination. It requires dedication, discipline, and a willingness to learn and adapt. But with the right guidance and mindset, you can achieve the financial freedom you desire.

Let's get started on your journey to financial independence!

Overview of Financial Independence

Financial independence is more than just a financial milestone; it's a lifestyle choice that allows you to live life on your own terms. This section will provide a clear definition of financial independence, outline its benefits, and address common misconceptions that might hold you back from achieving it.

Definition and Benefits

Definition of Financial Independence

Financial independence is the state of having sufficient personal wealth to live without having to work actively for basic necessities. In other words, your assets generate enough income to cover your living expenses. This can be achieved through a combination of savings, investments, and passive income sources.

Key Components of Financial Independence

- Savings: Regularly setting aside a portion of your income.

- Investments: Putting money into assets that generate returns over time, such as stocks, bonds, real estate, or mutual funds.

- Passive Income: Income generated with little to no ongoing effort, such as rental income, dividends, interest, or business income where you are not actively involved.

Benefits of Financial Independence

1. Freedom of Choice

- Career Flexibility: You can choose to work in a field you are passionate about without worrying about the paycheck. This freedom might also allow you to take a sabbatical, start your own business, or retire early.

- Lifestyle Options: Financial independence gives you the flexibility to live where you want, travel as you wish, and pursue hobbies and interests that enhance your life satisfaction.

2. Reduced Stress and Anxiety

- Financial Security: With a solid financial foundation, you can eliminate the constant worry about money, bills, and unexpected expenses. This security leads to better mental health and overall well-being.

- Emergency Preparedness: Having adequate savings and investments means you are better prepared for life's unexpected events, such as medical emergencies, job loss, or other crises.

3. Improved Quality of Life

  - Time Freedom: Financial independence allows you to spend more time with family and friends, pursue personal interests, volunteer, or simply relax. Time is a finite resource, and financial independence lets you use it in ways that bring you joy and satisfaction.

  - Health and Well-being: With financial security, you can afford to invest in your health by accessing better healthcare, eating healthier, and having more time to exercise and rest. Reducing financial stress also has positive effects on your physical health.

4. Personal Growth and Fulfillment

  - Pursuing Passions: Financial independence enables you to invest time and money in your passions and interests. Whether it's furthering your education, starting a new hobby, or traveling the world, financial freedom gives you the ability to pursue what makes you happy.

  - Continuous Learning: With financial security, you have the resources to continue learning and growing. This could mean taking courses, attending workshops, or simply having the time to read and explore new ideas.

5. Legacy and Impact

- Family Security: Financial independence allows you to provide for your family, ensuring that your loved ones are taken care of. You can fund your children's education, help family members in need, and leave a financial legacy.

- Charitable Giving: Financial independence enables you to give back to your community and support causes you care about. You can donate money, time, and resources to make a positive impact on the world.

Common Misconceptions

1. Financial Independence Means Being Rich

- Reality: Financial independence is not about having vast amounts of wealth; it's about having enough to cover your expenses without relying on active work. It's more about financial security and freedom rather than becoming wealthy.

2. You Need a High Income to Achieve Financial Independence

- Reality: While a high income can certainly help, it's not a requirement. Financial independence is more about managing your money wisely, living within your means, saving diligently, and investing effectively. Many people with moderate incomes achieve financial independence through disciplined saving and investing.

3. Financial Independence Requires Extreme Frugality

- Reality: Achieving financial independence doesn't mean you have to live a life of deprivation. It's about finding a balance between enjoying your life now and saving for the future. Smart budgeting, mindful spending, and making informed financial decisions are key.

4. It's Too Late to Start

- Reality: It's never too late to start working towards financial independence. While starting early gives you the advantage of time and compound interest, making positive financial changes at any stage of life can significantly improve your financial situation and help you move towards independence.

5. Financial Independence Means You Stop Working Entirely

- Reality: Financial independence gives you the choice to work or not. Many people choose to continue working because they enjoy it, but they do so on their own terms, without the financial necessity. It's about having the freedom to make that choice.

6. It's Only for Financial Experts

- Reality: Financial independence is achievable by anyone willing to learn and apply basic financial principles. You don't need to be a financial expert; you just need to be committed to your goals and willing to take the necessary steps.

By understanding the true meaning of financial independence, recognizing its broad benefits, and dispelling common misconceptions, you can approach your financial journey with confidence and clarity. This book will guide you through practical, actionable steps to help you achieve financial independence, tailored to your unique situation.

Chapter 1: Understanding Your Financial Situation

Achieving financial independence starts with a clear and honest understanding of your current financial situation. This involves evaluating your income, expenses, debts, and assets to create a comprehensive personal balance sheet. This chapter will guide you through the steps necessary to assess your finances accurately and set a solid foundation for your financial journey.

Assessing Your Current Finances

Evaluating Income

1. Identify All Income Sources

   - Primary Income: Document your salary or wages from your main job.

   - Secondary Income: Include any part-time jobs, freelance work, side hustles, or other sources of income.

   - Passive Income: Note any income from investments, rental properties, royalties, or other sources that generate income with minimal effort.

2. Calculate Total Monthly Income

   - Gross Income: Sum of all your income sources before any deductions.

- Net Income: Your take-home pay after taxes, insurance, retirement contributions, and other deductions.

Evaluating Expenses

1. Track Your Spending

- Daily Tracking: Keep a daily log of all expenses, no matter how small. Use a notebook, spreadsheet, or a budgeting app.

- Categorize Expenses: Group your spending into categories such as housing, utilities, groceries, transportation, entertainment, dining out, etc.

2. Monthly Expense Summary

- Fixed Expenses: Regular, predictable expenses such as rent or mortgage, utilities, car payments, insurance premiums, and loan payments.

- Variable Expenses: Fluctuating expenses like groceries, dining out, entertainment, and travel.

- Discretionary Spending: Non-essential spending on things like hobbies, subscriptions, and personal care.

3. Identify Patterns and Areas for Improvement

- Analyze Spending: Look for patterns in your spending and identify areas where you can cut back. Highlight unnecessary or excessive expenses.

Evaluating Debts

1. List All Debts

   - Types of Debts: Include credit card balances, student loans, car loans, mortgages, personal loans, and any other liabilities.

   - Details of Each Debt: Note the balance, interest rate, minimum monthly payment, and due date for each debt.

2. Calculate Total Debt

   - Total Debt Amount: Sum of all outstanding balances.

   - Monthly Debt Payments: Total of all minimum monthly payments required to service your debts.

3. Debt Analysis

   - Interest Rates: Identify high-interest debts that should be prioritized for repayment.

   - Debt-to-Income Ratio: Calculate your debt-to-income ratio by dividing your total monthly debt payments by your gross monthly income. A lower ratio indicates better financial health.

Evaluating Assets

1. Identify All Assets

   - Liquid Assets: Cash and cash equivalents, such as checking and savings accounts.

   - Investments: Stocks, bonds, mutual funds, retirement accounts (e.g., 401(k), IRA), and other investment accounts.

- Physical Assets: Real estate, vehicles, valuable personal property (jewelry, art, etc.).

   - Other Assets: Any other items of value that could be liquidated if necessary.

2. Calculate Net Worth

   - Total Assets: Sum of all your assets.

   - Total Liabilities: Sum of all your debts.

   - Net Worth: Subtract total liabilities from total assets. This number represents your financial standing at a given point in time.

3. Asset Analysis

   - Liquidity: Determine how easily your assets can be converted into cash. Liquid assets provide immediate financial flexibility.

   - Growth Potential: Assess the potential for your investments to grow over time and contribute to your long-term financial goals.

Creating a Personal Balance Sheet

A personal balance sheet is a snapshot of your financial situation, summarizing your income, expenses, debts, and assets. It provides a clear picture of where you stand financially and helps you track your progress over time.

Steps to Create a Personal Balance Sheet

1. Income Section

   - List All Income Sources: Document each source of income and its monthly amount.

   - Total Monthly Income: Sum all income sources to get your total monthly income.

2. Expense Section

   - Categorize Expenses: Break down your expenses into fixed, variable, and discretionary categories.

   - Monthly Expense Amounts: List the monthly amount for each expense category.

   - Total Monthly Expenses: Sum all expense categories to get your total monthly expenses.

3. Debt Section

   - List All Debts: Document each debt with its current balance, interest rate, and minimum monthly payment.

   - Total Debt: Sum the balances of all debts to get your total debt amount.

   - Total Monthly Debt Payments: Sum all minimum monthly payments required to service your debts.

4. Asset Section

   - List All Assets: Document each asset with its current value.

- Total Assets: Sum the values of all assets to get your total assets amount.

5. Net Worth Calculation

- Net Worth: Subtract total liabilities (debts) from total assets. This is your net worth.

Example Personal Balance Sheet

Chapter 1: Understanding Your Financial Situation

Achieving financial independence starts with a clear and honest understanding of your current financial situation. This involves evaluating your income, expenses, debts, and assets to create a comprehensive personal balance sheet. This chapter will guide you through the steps necessary to assess your finances accurately and set a solid foundation for your financial journey.

Assessing Your Current Finances

Evaluating Income

1. Identify All Income Sources

- Primary Income: Document your salary or wages from your main job.

- Secondary Income: Include any part-time jobs, freelance work, side hustles, or other sources of income.

- Passive Income: Note any income from investments, rental properties, royalties, or other sources that generate income with minimal effort.

2. Calculate Total Monthly Income

- Gross Income: Sum of all your income sources before any deductions.

- Net Income: Your take-home pay after taxes, insurance, retirement contributions, and other deductions.

Evaluating Expenses

1. Track Your Spending

- Daily Tracking: Keep a daily log of all expenses, no matter how small. Use a notebook, spreadsheet, or a budgeting app.

- Categorize Expenses: Group your spending into categories such as housing, utilities, groceries, transportation, entertainment, dining out, etc.

2. Monthly Expense Summary

- Fixed Expenses: Regular, predictable expenses such as rent or mortgage, utilities, car payments, insurance premiums, and loan payments.

- Variable Expenses: Fluctuating expenses like groceries, dining out, entertainment, and travel.

- Discretionary Spending: Non-essential spending on things like hobbies, subscriptions, and personal care.

3. Identify Patterns and Areas for Improvement

- Analyze Spending: Look for patterns in your spending and identify areas where you can cut back. Highlight unnecessary or excessive expenses.

Evaluating Debts

1. List All Debts

- Types of Debts: Include credit card balances, student loans, car loans, mortgages, personal loans, and any other liabilities.

- Details of Each Debt: Note the balance, interest rate, minimum monthly payment, and due date for each debt.

2. Calculate Total Debt

- Total Debt Amount: Sum of all outstanding balances.

- Monthly Debt Payments: Total of all minimum monthly payments required to service your debts.

3. Debt Analysis

- Interest Rates: Identify high-interest debts that should be prioritized for repayment.

- Debt-to-Income Ratio: Calculate your debt-to-income ratio by dividing your total monthly debt payments by your gross monthly income. A lower ratio indicates better financial health.

Evaluating Assets

1. Identify All Assets

   - Liquid Assets: Cash and cash equivalents, such as checking and savings accounts.

   - Investments: Stocks, bonds, mutual funds, retirement accounts (e.g., 401(k), IRA), and other investment accounts.

   - Physical Assets: Real estate, vehicles, valuable personal property (jewelry, art, etc.).

   - Other Assets: Any other items of value that could be liquidated if necessary.

2. Calculate Net Worth

   - Total Assets: Sum of all your assets.

   - Total Liabilities: Sum of all your debts.

   - Net Worth: Subtract total liabilities from total assets. This number represents your financial standing at a given point in time.

3. Asset Analysis

   - Liquidity: Determine how easily your assets can be converted into cash. Liquid assets provide immediate financial flexibility.

- Growth Potential: Assess the potential for your investments to grow over time and contribute to your long-term financial goals.

Creating a Personal Balance Sheet

A personal balance sheet is a snapshot of your financial situation, summarizing your income, expenses, debts, and assets. It provides a clear picture of where you stand financially and helps you track your progress over time.

Steps to Create a Personal Balance Sheet

1. Income Section

   - List All Income Sources: Document each source of income and its monthly amount.

   - Total Monthly Income: Sum all income sources to get your total monthly income.

2. Expense Section

   - Categorize Expenses: Break down your expenses into fixed, variable, and discretionary categories.

   - Monthly Expense Amounts: List the monthly amount for each expense category.

- Total Monthly Expenses: Sum all expense categories to get your total monthly expenses.

3. Debt Section

   - List All Debts: Document each debt with its current balance, interest rate, and minimum monthly payment.

   - Total Debt: Sum the balances of all debts to get your total debt amount.

   - Total Monthly Debt Payments: Sum all minimum monthly payments required to service your debts.

4. Asset Section

   - List All Assets: Document each asset with its current value.

   - Total Assets: Sum the values of all assets to get your total assets amount.

5. Net Worth Calculation

   - Net Worth: Subtract total liabilities (debts) from total assets. This is your net worth.

Example Personal Balance Sheet

| Income | Monthly Amount |

Income	Amount
Primary Job	$3,500
Freelance Work	$500
Investment Income	$200
Total Income	$4,200

Expenses	Monthly Amount
Rent	$1,200
Utilities	$200
Groceries	$400
Car Payment	$300
Insurance	$150
Entertainment	$100
Dining Out	$150
Total Expenses	$2,500

Debts	Balance	Monthly Payment
Credit Card	$3,000	$100
Student Loan	$15,000	$150
Car Loan	$10,000	$300

| Total Debt | $28,000 | $550 |

Assets	Current Value
Checking Account	$2,000
Savings Account	$5,000
Investment Account	$10,000
Car	$8,000
Total Assets	$25,000

Net Worth	
Total Assets	$25,000
Total Liabilities	$28,000
Net Worth	-$3,000

Practical Steps to Assess Your Finances

1. Gather Financial Documents

   - Collect pay stubs, bank statements, credit card statements, loan documents, investment account statements, and bills.

2. Use Financial Tools

- Utilize budgeting apps, spreadsheets, or financial software to organize and track your financial data.

3. Regular Review

- Schedule a monthly review of your finances to update your balance sheet and adjust your budget as needed.

4. Seek Professional Help

- If necessary, consult a financial advisor to help you understand and improve your financial situation.

By thoroughly assessing your current finances and creating a detailed personal balance sheet, you lay the groundwork for setting achievable financial goals and creating a strategic plan to reach financial independence. This comprehensive understanding will empower you to make informed decisions and take control of your financial future.

Chapter 1: Understanding Your Financial Situation

Setting a Baseline: Establishing Your Starting Point

Before embarking on your journey to financial independence, it's essential to establish your starting point. This involves taking stock of your current financial situation, identifying your financial goals, and understanding the gap between where you are and where you want to be. Setting a baseline allows you to create a roadmap for success and track your progress along the way.

Assessing Your Current Financial Situation

1. Review Your Finances: Gather all relevant financial documents, including bank statements, bills, pay stubs, and investment statements.

2. Calculate Your Net Worth: Subtract your liabilities (debts) from your assets to determine your net worth. This provides a snapshot of your overall financial health.

3. Analyze Your Cash Flow: Review your income and expenses to understand your spending habits and identify areas for improvement.

4. Evaluate Your Debt: Make a list of all your debts, including balances, interest rates, and minimum monthly payments. This will help you prioritize debt repayment strategies.

5. Assess Your Savings and Investments: Review your savings accounts, retirement accounts, and investment portfolios to determine your current level of savings and investment growth.

Identifying Your Financial Goals

1. Short-Term Goals: Identify specific financial milestones you want to achieve within the next 1-3 years, such as building an emergency fund or paying off high-interest debt.

2. Medium-Term Goals: Define goals you want to accomplish within the next 3-5 years, such as saving for a down payment on a home or funding a major purchase.

3. Long-Term Goals: Determine your long-term financial aspirations, such as retiring early, traveling the world, or achieving financial independence.

Understanding the Gap

1. Quantify the Discrepancy: Calculate the gap between your current financial situation and your desired financial goals. This will help you understand what needs to be done to bridge the divide.

2. Identify Obstacles: Identify any obstacles or challenges that may prevent you from reaching your financial goals, such as excessive debt, low income, or lack of savings discipline.

3. Develop Strategies: Brainstorm strategies to overcome obstacles and close the gap between your current situation and your desired outcome. This may involve increasing income, reducing expenses, or improving investment returns.

Creating a Roadmap

1. Prioritize Goals: Rank your financial goals based on importance and feasibility. Focus on addressing immediate needs while also planning for the future.

2. Set Specific Targets: Establish measurable targets for each goal, including timelines and benchmarks for success.

3. Develop Action Plans: Break down each goal into actionable steps and develop a plan for achieving them. Assign responsibilities, set deadlines, and track progress regularly.

4. Monitor and Adjust: Continuously monitor your progress towards your financial goals and adjust your plans as needed. Be flexible and willing to adapt to changing circumstances.

Conclusion

Setting a baseline for your financial journey is a crucial first step towards achieving financial independence. By understanding your current financial situation, identifying your goals, and developing a roadmap for success, you can take control of your finances and work towards a more secure and prosperous future. Remember, financial independence is attainable with dedication, discipline, and strategic planning.

Chapter 2: Setting Clear Financial Goals

Importance of Goals: Why Setting Financial Goals is Crucial

Setting financial goals is the cornerstone of achieving financial independence and overall financial health. Clear, well-defined goals provide direction, motivation, and a benchmark for measuring progress. This chapter delves into why setting financial goals is essential and how it can transform your financial future.

Why Setting Financial Goals is Crucial

1. Provides Direction and Focus

Clarity of Purpose: Financial goals give you a clear sense of purpose. They define what you are working towards and help prioritize your financial decisions.

Guidance for Decision-Making: With specific goals in mind, you can make informed decisions about spending, saving, and investing that align with your objectives.

2. Motivates and Inspires

Encourages Discipline: Knowing what you are working towards helps cultivate discipline in managing your finances. It encourages you to stick to your budget and savings plan.

Boosts Motivation: Seeing progress towards your goals can be highly motivating. Each milestone reached serves as a reminder of your ability to achieve your financial dreams.

3. Enhances Financial Control

Budgeting Efficiency: Goals enable you to create a budget that reflects your priorities. This ensures that your money is allocated towards what matters most.

Spending Awareness: When you have specific targets, you become more conscious of your spending habits. This awareness helps prevent impulsive purchases and wasteful spending.

4. Facilitates Measurement and Tracking

Progress Monitoring: Clear goals provide benchmarks against which you can measure your progress. This helps you stay on track and make adjustments as needed.

Accountability: Regularly tracking your progress keeps you accountable to yourself. It allows you to see how far you've come and what more needs to be done.

5. Reduces Financial Stress

Preparedness for Emergencies: Setting goals often includes building an emergency fund. This preparedness can significantly reduce financial anxiety.

Long-Term Security: Goals like retirement savings and debt reduction contribute to long-term financial security, providing peace of mind.

6. Promotes Smart Financial Habits

Savings and Investment Discipline: Goals encourage regular saving and investing. Over time, these habits can lead to substantial financial growth.

Debt Management: Specific goals related to debt repayment can help you develop strategies to eliminate debt efficiently, reducing the overall cost of borrowing.

7. Enables Future Planning

Life Milestones: Goals can be tailored to significant life events such as buying a home, funding education, or starting a business. Planning for these milestones ensures you are financially prepared when the time comes.

Retirement Planning: Setting retirement goals ensures that you save and invest adequately to enjoy a comfortable retirement.

Practical Steps to Setting Financial Goals

Identify Your Priorities

Short-Term Goals: Focus on immediate financial needs, such as building an emergency fund, paying off high-interest debt, or saving for a specific purchase.

Medium-Term Goals: These might include saving for a down payment on a house, funding education, or purchasing a car.

Long-Term Goals: Long-term goals often involve retirement planning, wealth building, and achieving financial independence.

Be Specific and Realistic

SMART Goals: Ensure your goals are Specific, Measurable, Achievable, Relevant, and Time-bound. This framework helps create clear and actionable goals.

Realistic Expectations: Set goals that are challenging yet attainable. Overly ambitious goals can lead to frustration and disappointment.

Break Down Goals into Manageable Steps

Milestones: Divide larger goals into smaller, manageable milestones. This makes the process less overwhelming and allows for regular progress checks.

Action Plans: Develop detailed action plans for each goal, outlining the steps needed to achieve them.

Regularly Review and Adjust Goals

Progress Assessment: Regularly assess your progress towards each goal. Make adjustments as necessary to stay on track.

Adapt to Changes: Life circumstances can change, impacting your financial situation. Be flexible and adjust your goals to reflect these changes.

Conclusion

Setting financial goals is not just about envisioning your future; it's about taking concrete steps to shape it. By providing direction, motivation, and a clear framework for tracking progress, financial goals are integral to achieving financial independence and long-term security. This chapter underscores the importance of goal setting and offers practical steps to help you define and reach your financial objectives.

Chapter 2: Setting Clear Financial Goals

SMART Goals: How to Set Specific, Measurable, Achievable, Relevant, and Time-bound Goals

Setting SMART goals is a powerful technique to enhance the clarity and effectiveness of your financial planning. SMART is an acronym that stands for Specific, Measurable, Achievable, Relevant, and Time-bound. By following this framework, you can create well-defined goals that are easier to achieve and track. This section will guide you through the process of setting SMART financial goals.

Specific

Define Your Goal Clearly

Details Matter: Ensure your goal is precise and unambiguous. Instead of a vague goal like "save money," specify the exact amount you want to save and for what purpose.

Examples:

"Save $5,000 for an emergency fund."

"Pay off $2,000 of credit card debt."

Identify the Purpose

Why It Matters: Understanding the reason behind your goal provides motivation. Explain why this goal is important to you.

Examples:

"Save $5,000 for an emergency fund to cover unexpected expenses without going into debt."

"Pay off $2,000 of credit card debt to improve my credit score and reduce interest payments."

Measurable

Set Criteria for Success

Quantifiable Metrics: Ensure your goal includes criteria that allow you to track progress and know when you've achieved it.

Examples:

"Save $500 per month to reach $5,000 in 10 months."

"Pay an extra $200 per month on my credit card to pay off $2,000 in 10 months."

Use Tools for Tracking

Financial Software and Apps: Utilize budgeting apps or spreadsheets to monitor your progress regularly.

Examples:

"Use a budgeting app to track monthly savings towards my $5,000 goal."

"Update a debt repayment spreadsheet each month to ensure I'm on track to pay off $2,000."

Achievable

Set Realistic Goals

Assess Your Current Situation: Ensure your goal is realistic given your financial situation and constraints. Avoid setting goals that are too ambitious and unattainable.

Examples:

"Based on my current income and expenses, saving $500 per month is feasible."

"I can afford to pay an extra $200 per month on my credit card debt without compromising essential expenses."

Consider Resources and Constraints

Availability of Resources: Account for any additional resources or support you might need to achieve your goal.

Examples:

"I will cut down on dining out and entertainment to free up $500 for savings each month."

"I will generate extra income through freelancing to cover the additional $200 debt payment."

Relevant

Align with Your Long-Term Objectives

Personal Relevance: Ensure your goal is relevant to your broader financial and life objectives. It should be meaningful and worthwhile.

Examples:

"Building an emergency fund aligns with my goal of achieving financial stability and independence."

"Paying off credit card debt supports my objective of improving my financial health and reducing stress."

Prioritize Accordingly

Immediate vs. Future Needs: Balance your goals based on immediate financial needs and future aspirations.

Examples:

"Prioritizing an emergency fund now will prevent financial setbacks in the future."

"Reducing high-interest debt will free up funds for future investments and savings."

Time-bound

Set a Deadline

Specific Time Frames: Define a clear deadline for achieving your goal to create a sense of urgency and maintain focus.

Examples:

"Save $5,000 for an emergency fund within 10 months."

"Pay off $2,000 of credit card debt within 10 months."

Break Down into Milestones

Intermediate Targets: Divide your goal into smaller, time-bound milestones to make it more manageable and track able.

Examples:

"Save $500 per month to reach $5,000 in 10 months. Review savings progress monthly."

"Pay an extra $200 per month on my credit card to pay off $2,000 in 10 months. Check debt balance monthly."

Practical Examples of SMART Financial Goals

Emergency Fund

Specific: "Save $5,000 for an emergency fund."

Measurable: "Save $500 per month."

Achievable: "Cut back on non-essential spending to save $500 monthly."

Relevant: "An emergency fund is crucial for financial security."

Time-bound: "Save $5,000 within 10 months."

Debt Repayment

Specific: "Pay off $2,000 of credit card debt."

Measurable: "Pay an extra $200 per month."

Achievable: "Allocate extra income from freelancing to debt repayment."

Relevant: "Reducing debt improves my financial health."

Time-bound: "Pay off $2,000 within 10 months."

Retirement Savings

Specific: "Contribute $10,000 to my retirement account."

Measurable: "Contribute $833 per month."

Achievable: "Increase automatic monthly contributions by adjusting my budget."

Relevant: "Enhancing retirement savings ensures long-term financial security."

Time-bound: "Achieve this within 12 months."

Conclusion

Setting SMART financial goals ensures that your objectives are clear, realistic, and achievable within a specified timeframe. By following the SMART framework, you can create a detailed roadmap to financial success, making it easier to track progress and stay motivated. This structured approach to goal-setting will significantly enhance your chances of achieving financial independence and long-term financial well-being.

Chapter 3: Budgeting Basics

1. Creating a Budget

Creating a budget is the foundation of financial management. A well-crafted budget helps you control your spending, save for future goals, and ensure you live within your means. This section provides a step-by-step guide to creating a simple and effective budget.

Step-by-Step Guide to Creating a Simple Budget

Step 1: Gather Financial Information

Collect Income Information

List all sources of income, including salary, freelance work, investments, and any other sources.

Use net income (after taxes and deductions) for accurate budgeting.

Track Expenses

Review bank statements, credit card bills, and receipts from the past few months.

Categorize expenses into fixed (rent, utilities) and variable (groceries, entertainment).

Step 2: List Monthly Income and Expenses

Monthly Income

Sum up all sources of monthly income to get your total monthly income.

Monthly Expenses

Fixed Expenses: These are regular, recurring expenses such as rent/mortgage, utilities, car payments, insurance, and loan payments.

Variable Expenses: These fluctuate monthly and include groceries, dining out, entertainment, travel, and personal care.

Irregular Expenses: Expenses that occur periodically but not monthly, like car maintenance or medical bills. Estimate a monthly amount to set aside.

Step 3: Categorize and Prioritize Expenses

Essential Expenses

Fixed and necessary costs like housing, utilities, groceries, transportation, insurance, and debt payments.

Consider these non-negotiable as they cover basic needs and obligations.

Discretionary Expenses

Non-essential spending like dining out, entertainment, hobbies, and luxury items.

These can be adjusted or reduced if needed to balance the budget.

Step 4: Set Financial Goals

Short-Term Goals

Objectives to achieve within the next 1-2 years, like building an emergency fund or paying off a specific debt.

Allocate a portion of your budget towards these goals.

Long-Term Goals

Goals that span over several years, such as retirement savings, buying a home, or funding education.

Establish regular contributions towards these goals in your budget.

Step 5: Allocate Income to Expenses and Goals

Assign Income to Expense Categories

Distribute your total income to cover all fixed and variable expenses first.

Ensure essential expenses are fully covered before allocating funds to discretionary spending.

Savings and Debt Repayment

Prioritize savings and debt repayment within your budget.

Aim for at least 20% of your income to go towards savings and debt reduction if possible.

Adjust and Balance

If expenses exceed income, review discretionary spending for possible cuts.

Adjust allocations to ensure that your budget is balanced and you are not spending more than you earn.

Step 6: Implement and Monitor Your Budget

Track Spending

Use budgeting apps, spreadsheets, or financial software to track your expenses against your budget.

Record transactions daily or weekly to stay on top of your spending.

Review Regularly

Conduct monthly budget reviews to compare actual spending with your planned budget.

Identify areas where you are over or under budget and adjust accordingly.

Adjust as Needed

Life changes and unexpected expenses may require adjustments to your budget.

Be flexible and update your budget to reflect changes in income or expenses.

Step 7: Maintain Discipline and Stay Motivated

Stick to Your Plan

Follow your budget closely and resist the temptation to overspend.

Use reminders or alerts to stay on track with your financial commitments.

Celebrate Milestones

Acknowledge and celebrate small victories and milestones achieved through disciplined budgeting.

This helps maintain motivation and commitment to your financial goals.

Practical Example of a Simple Monthly Budget

Monthly Income: $3,500

Expenses:

Fixed Expenses:

Rent/Mortgage: $1,000

Utilities: $150

Car Payment: $300

Insurance: $200

Loan Payments: $250

Variable Expenses:

Groceries: $400

Dining Out: $150

Entertainment: $100

Transportation: $100

Personal Care: $50

Savings and Debt Repayment:

Emergency Fund: $200

Retirement Savings: $300

Extra Debt Payments: $100

Total Expenses: $3,300

Surplus: $200 (to be allocated to savings or future goals)

Conclusion

Creating a budget is a fundamental step towards achieving financial stability and independence. By following this step-by-step guide, you can develop a budget that aligns with your financial goals, ensures essential expenses are covered, and allows you to save for the future. Regularly monitoring and adjusting your budget will help you stay on track and make informed financial decisions.

Chapter 3: Budgeting Basics

2. Tracking Expenses

Effectively tracking your expenses is crucial for maintaining control over your finances and adhering to your budget. This section explores various methods for tracking expenses on a daily, weekly, and monthly basis to ensure you stay on top of your financial situation.

Methods for Tracking Daily, Weekly, and Monthly Expenses

Daily Expense Tracking

Manual Tracking

Notebook or Journal: Carry a small notebook or journal to jot down every purchase you make throughout the day. This method is straightforward and helps you stay mindful of your spending.

Receipts: Collect receipts for all purchases and record the amounts in your notebook or an expense tracking sheet at the end of each day.

Digital Tools

Expense Tracking Apps: Use apps like Mint, YNAB (You Need A Budget), PocketGuard, or Expensify. These apps allow you to log expenses in real-time and categorize them automatically.

Spreadsheets: Create a simple Excel or Google Sheets document where you enter expenses daily. Use categories to organize your spending for easier analysis.

Envelope System

Cash Envelopes: Allocate cash for different spending categories (e.g., groceries, dining out) and place the cash in labeled envelopes. Once an envelope is empty, you know you've reached your limit for that category.

Weekly Expense Tracking

Review and Reconcile

Weekly Review: Set aside time each week to review your expenses. Compare your recorded expenses against your budget to identify any discrepancies or overspending.

Reconcile Accounts: Ensure that your bank account and credit card statements match your recorded expenses. This helps catch any errors or unauthorized transactions.

Categorization

Expense Categories: Organize your expenses into categories such as housing, transportation, food, entertainment, and savings. This provides a clear picture of where your money is going.

Analyze Trends: Look for patterns in your spending. Are there any categories where you consistently overspend? Identifying these trends helps you make necessary adjustments.

Adjust Budget Allocations

Flexible Adjustments: If you notice that certain categories are consistently over or under budget, adjust your budget allocations for the coming week. This flexibility ensures your budget remains realistic and achievable.

Monthly Expense Tracking

Comprehensive Review

Monthly Summary: At the end of each month, compile a summary of all your expenses. Review your total spending for each category and compare it to your budget.

Evaluate Progress: Assess your progress towards your financial goals. Are you saving as much as planned? Have you stayed within your budget limits?

Detailed Analysis

Expense Reports: Generate detailed reports using expense tracking apps or spreadsheets. These reports can show you trends over time and highlight areas for improvement.

Identify Savings Opportunities: Look for opportunities to reduce expenses or increase savings. This might include cutting back on non-essential spending or finding cheaper alternatives for regular purchases.

Set Goals for the Next Month

Adjust Budget: Based on your analysis, adjust your budget for the next month. Allocate funds to areas where you need more and reduce allocations for categories where you've overspent.

Set New Goals: Establish new short-term financial goals for the upcoming month. These might include paying down debt, increasing savings, or reducing discretionary spending.

Practical Tools and Techniques

Budgeting Apps

Mint: Tracks expenses, creates budgets, and provides financial insights.

YNAB (You Need A Budget): Focuses on proactive budgeting and assigning every dollar a job.

PocketGuard: Helps track spending and shows how much money is available after bills and savings goals.

Spreadsheets

Excel or Google Sheets: Use templates or create custom sheets to track income, expenses, and savings. Include columns for categories, dates, and amounts.

Formulas and Charts: Utilize spreadsheet formulas to sum expenses and create charts to visualize spending patterns.

Bank and Credit Card Alerts

Automatic Alerts: Set up alerts for transactions, low balances, or unusual spending. This helps you stay informed about your financial activity in real-time.

Receipts and Statements

Keep Receipts: Store receipts in a designated folder or use a receipt scanning app to digitize them. This provides a backup for tracking and verifying expenses.

Monthly Statements: Review your bank and credit card statements monthly to ensure all recorded transactions are accurate.

Tips for Effective Expense Tracking

Be Consistent

Track your expenses daily or at least weekly to avoid backlog and ensure accuracy.

Make it a routine part of your day or week to maintain consistency.

Be Honest

Record every expense, no matter how small. This helps you get a true picture of your spending habits.

Avoid rounding amounts; record the exact figures.

Stay Organized

Use categories and subcategories to organize your expenses. This makes it easier to analyze and identify areas for improvement.

Keep your tracking tools (notebooks, apps, spreadsheets) updated and accessible.

Review Regularly

Regularly review your expense reports and budget to make necessary adjustments.

Use insights from your tracking to refine your spending habits and financial goals.

Conclusion

Tracking expenses is a vital part of effective budgeting and financial management. By implementing daily, weekly, and monthly tracking methods, you can maintain control over your finances, identify areas for improvement, and stay aligned with your financial goals. Consistent and honest tracking, combined with regular reviews and adjustments, will help you achieve financial stability and independence.

Chapter 3: Budgeting Basics

3. Adjusting Your Budget

Creating a budget is just the first step in effective financial management. To ensure it remains relevant and effective, regular adjustments are necessary. This section covers how to tweak your budget to stay on track and achieve your financial goals.

How to Tweak Your Budget to Stay on Track

1. Regularly Review Your Budget

Monthly Reviews

Set a Schedule: Dedicate time at the end of each month to review your budget. This helps you stay aware of your financial situation and make timely adjustments.

Compare Actual vs. Budgeted Amounts: Look at your actual spending and compare it to your budgeted amounts for each category. Identify any discrepancies.

Quarterly and Annual Reviews

Assess Trends: Review your budget on a quarterly and annual basis to identify long-term trends. This helps in understanding seasonal expenses or changes in income and spending patterns.

Adjust Long-Term Goals: Use these reviews to adjust your long-term financial goals based on your progress and any changes in circumstances.

2. Identify Areas for Adjustment

Analyze Spending Patterns

Over and Under Budget: Identify categories where you consistently overspend or underspend. This can help you make necessary adjustments to your budget.

Unplanned Expenses: Look for any unexpected or unplanned expenses. Determine if these are one-time occurrences or if they should be accounted for in your budget.

Prioritize Spending

Essential vs. Non-Essential: Differentiate between essential and non-essential expenses. Ensure that essential expenses are fully covered before allocating funds to non-essential categories.

Flexible Categories: Identify categories that can be adjusted. For instance, if you overspend on dining out, you can reduce spending in another discretionary category to balance it out.

3. Make Necessary Adjustments

Reallocate Funds

Shift Money Between Categories: If you find that some categories are consistently over budget while others are under budget, reallocate funds to better match your actual spending patterns.

Adjust Savings Goals: If you have more or less money than expected, adjust your savings goals accordingly. Increase savings if you have a surplus, or reduce savings goals temporarily if needed.

Update Income and Expense Projections

Reflect Changes in Income: If your income changes, such as receiving a raise or losing a source of income, update your budget to reflect this. Adjust your spending and savings plans based on your new income level.

Account for New Expenses: Include any new regular expenses in your budget. This might include new subscriptions, increased utility costs, or additional debt repayments.

4. Utilize Budgeting Tools

Budgeting Apps and Software

Automated Adjustments: Many budgeting apps allow for easy adjustments. Use features like automatic categorization and real-time updates to streamline the process.

Spending Alerts: Set up alerts for overspending in certain categories. This can help you make adjustments before you exceed your budget significantly.

Spreadsheets

Dynamic Templates: Use spreadsheet templates that allow for easy adjustments. Make use of formulas to automatically update totals as you input new data.

Scenario Planning: Create multiple budget scenarios to plan for different financial situations. This can help you prepare for changes in income or unexpected expenses.

5. Implement and Monitor Changes

Test Adjustments

Trial Period: Implement adjustments on a trial basis. Monitor the impact on your overall budget and financial goals.

Feedback Loop: Regularly review the effectiveness of your adjustments. If they're not working as expected, be ready to make further changes.

Maintain Flexibility

Adapt to Life Changes: Be prepared to adjust your budget as your life circumstances change. This includes changes in employment, family dynamics, health, or major purchases.

Emergency Adjustments: Have a plan for making quick adjustments in case of emergencies, such as unexpected medical expenses or urgent home repairs.

6. Communicate and Collaborate

Family or Partner Involvement

Shared Budgeting: If you share finances with a partner or family, ensure that everyone is involved in the budgeting process. Regularly communicate about financial goals and adjustments.

Collective Decisions: Make budget adjustments collaboratively to ensure that all parties are on the same page and committed to the plan.

Seek Professional Advice

Financial Advisors: If you're struggling to manage your budget or need help with significant adjustments, consider consulting a financial advisor. They can provide personalized advice and strategies.

Practical Examples of Budget Adjustments

Example 1: Reducing Discretionary Spending

Current Scenario: Monthly dining out budget is $300, but you consistently spend $400.

Adjustment: Reduce entertainment budget by $100 to cover the excess dining out expenses. Alternatively, set a stricter limit on dining out by planning meals at home.

Example 2: Increasing Savings

Current Scenario: You receive an unexpected bonus of $1,000.

Adjustment: Allocate 50% ($500) to your emergency fund, 30% ($300) to pay off debt, and 20% ($200) for a small personal reward or discretionary spending.

Example 3: Managing Increased Utility Costs

Current Scenario: Utility bills increase by $50 per month.

Adjustment: Reduce the clothing budget by $20 and the entertainment budget by $30 to cover the increased utility costs.

Conclusion

Adjusting your budget is an ongoing process that helps you stay aligned with your financial goals and adapt to changes in your financial situation. Regular reviews, careful analysis, and proactive adjustments ensure that your budget remains a useful tool for managing your finances. By following these steps, you can maintain control over your spending, optimize your savings, and achieve long-term financial stability and independence.

Chapter 4: Saving Strategies for Everyone

1. Building an Emergency Fund

Importance of Having a Safety Net

An emergency fund is a critical component of financial stability and independence. It serves as a safety net to cover unexpected expenses and financial emergencies, ensuring that you can navigate unforeseen circumstances without derailing your financial goals. Here, we explore the importance of having an emergency fund and how to build one effectively.

Why an Emergency Fund Matters

Financial Security

Protection Against Unexpected Expenses: Life is unpredictable, and unexpected expenses can arise at any time, such as medical emergencies, car repairs, or home maintenance. An emergency fund provides a buffer to handle these costs without relying on credit cards or loans, which can lead to debt.

Peace of Mind: Knowing you have a financial cushion can significantly reduce stress and anxiety. This peace of mind allows you to focus on other aspects of your life, such as career development, personal growth, and long-term financial planning.

Preventing Debt

Avoiding High-Interest Loans: Without an emergency fund, you might be forced to take out high-interest loans or use credit cards to cover unexpected expenses. This can quickly lead to a cycle of debt that is difficult to escape.

Maintaining Financial Health: An emergency fund helps you stay on track with your financial goals by preventing the need to divert funds from other savings or investment accounts.

Job Security and Income Stability

Cushion During Job Loss: Job loss or a reduction in income can be financially devastating. An emergency fund provides the necessary funds to cover living expenses while you search for new employment or adjust to reduced income.

Negotiation Power: Having a financial cushion allows you to make better career decisions without the pressure of immediate financial need. You can take the time to find a job that fits your career goals rather than accepting the first offer out of necessity.

Flexibility and Opportunities

Taking Advantage of Opportunities: Sometimes, opportunities require a financial outlay, such as further education, starting a business, or investing in a promising venture. An emergency fund gives you the flexibility to seize these opportunities without jeopardizing your financial stability.

Life Changes: Major life events, such as moving to a new city, starting a family, or dealing with a medical condition, can come with significant costs. An emergency fund ensures that you are prepared for these changes without financial strain.

How to Build an Emergency Fund

Set a Realistic Goal

Determine Your Target Amount: A common recommendation is to save three to six months' worth of living expenses. However, the ideal amount depends on your individual circumstances, such as job stability, income level, and personal financial obligations.

Start Small: If saving three to six months' worth of expenses feels overwhelming, start with a smaller goal, such as $500 or $1,000. Gradually increase your target as your savings habits improve.

Create a Separate Savings Account

Dedicated Account: Open a separate savings account specifically for your emergency fund. This keeps your emergency savings distinct from other funds and reduces the temptation to use the money for non-emergency expenses.

High-Interest Savings Account: Consider using a high-interest savings account to maximize the growth of your emergency fund. While the primary goal is accessibility, earning some interest on your savings is beneficial.

Automate Your Savings

Automatic Transfers: Set up automatic transfers from your checking account to your emergency fund savings account. This ensures consistent contributions without the need for manual intervention.

Payroll Deductions: If your employer offers direct deposit, allocate a portion of your paycheck to go directly into your emergency fund. This makes saving effortless and consistent.

Reduce Expenses and Increase Income

Cut Unnecessary Spending: Review your budget to identify areas where you can cut back on non-essential expenses. Redirect these funds to your emergency savings.

Supplemental Income: Consider taking on a side job or freelance work to boost your income. Use any extra earnings to accelerate your emergency fund savings.

Regularly Review and Adjust

Monitor Your Progress: Regularly review your emergency fund to ensure you are on track to meet your goal. Adjust your savings rate if necessary to stay on target.

Reevaluate Your Goal: Periodically reassess your emergency fund target to account for changes in your financial situation, such as increased living expenses, changes in employment, or new financial obligations.

Practical Example

Let's consider Jane, a freelance graphic designer, who wants to build an emergency fund. Her monthly living expenses are $3,000, including rent, utilities, groceries, transportation, and insurance. Jane decides to aim for six months' worth of expenses, totaling $18,000.

Set a Realistic Goal: Jane starts with an initial goal of saving $1,000 within the first three months.

Create a Separate Savings Account: She opens a high-interest savings account dedicated to her emergency fund.

Automate Your Savings: Jane sets up an automatic transfer of $500 from her checking account to her emergency fund each month.

Reduce Expenses and Increase Income: She reviews her budget and cuts back on dining out and subscription services, redirecting an additional $200 per month to her emergency fund. Jane also takes on extra freelance projects, contributing the extra income to her savings.

Regularly Review and Adjust: Jane monitors her progress monthly, celebrating small milestones and adjusting her savings rate as her income fluctuates.

By following these steps, Jane steadily builds her emergency fund, achieving her initial goal of $1,000 and then progressing towards her ultimate target of $18,000. This financial cushion provides her with security and peace of mind, knowing she is prepared for unexpected expenses or income disruptions.

Conclusion

An emergency fund is an essential part of financial planning that provides security, prevents debt, and offers flexibility in the face of life's uncertainties. By setting a realistic goal, creating a dedicated savings account, automating contributions, reducing expenses, and regularly reviewing progress, you can build a robust emergency fund. This safety net ensures you are prepared for unexpected financial challenges, contributing to long-term financial stability and independence.

Chapter 4: Saving Strategies for Everyone

2. Automatic Savings

Setting Up Automatic Transfers to Savings Accounts

Automatic savings is a powerful and straightforward strategy to build your savings consistently without having to remember to set aside money manually each month. By automating the process, you ensure that your savings goals are met effortlessly, which helps you stay disciplined and reduces the temptation to spend money intended for savings.

Benefits of Automatic Savings

Consistency

Regular Contributions: Automated transfers ensure that you consistently save a portion of your income, making it easier to reach your financial goals.

Habit Formation: Over time, automatic savings help you develop a strong savings habit, as the process becomes routine and integrated into your financial management.

Convenience

Set and Forget: Once you set up automatic transfers, the process requires no further effort on your part. This is particularly useful for individuals with busy schedules or those who struggle with manual saving.

Reduced Temptation: By automating your savings, you minimize the temptation to spend the money, as it is transferred out of your checking account before you have a chance to use it.

Financial Discipline

Prioritizing Savings: Automatic transfers prioritize your savings by treating them as a mandatory expense, ensuring that you save before spending on discretionary items.

Goal Achievement: This method helps you stay on track to achieve your financial goals, whether it's building an emergency fund, saving for a down payment on a house, or investing for retirement.

How to Set Up Automatic Transfers to Savings Accounts

Choose the Right Savings Account

High-Interest Savings Account: Select a savings account that offers a competitive interest rate to maximize your earnings. Online banks often provide higher interest rates than traditional brick-and-mortar banks.

Separate Accounts for Different Goals: Consider opening multiple savings accounts for different goals, such as an emergency fund, travel fund, or home down payment. This helps you stay organized and track progress towards each goal individually.

Determine Your Savings Goals

Short-Term Goals: Identify short-term savings goals you want to achieve within the next 1-2 years, such as building an emergency fund or saving for a vacation.

Long-Term Goals: Establish long-term savings goals, like retirement, buying a home, or funding education. Allocate a portion of your savings towards these goals.

Calculate How Much to Save

Percentage of Income: Decide on a percentage of your income to save each month. A common recommendation is to save at least 20% of your income, but this can vary based on your financial situation and goals.

Fixed Amount: Alternatively, you can set a fixed dollar amount to transfer each month. Ensure this amount fits comfortably within your budget to avoid financial strain.

Set Up Automatic Transfers

Online Banking: Log into your online banking account and navigate to the section for setting up transfers. Most banks have a feature for automatic or recurring transfers.

Transfer Details: Specify the amount you want to transfer, the frequency (e.g., weekly, bi-weekly, or monthly), and the date when the transfer should occur. For example, you might set up a transfer for the day after you receive your paycheck.

Account Information: Enter the details of the accounts involved, including the checking account from which the funds will be transferred and the savings account that will receive the funds.

Monitor and Adjust

Regular Reviews: Periodically review your automatic savings plan to ensure it aligns with your current financial situation and goals. Adjust the amount or frequency of transfers if your income changes or if you have new financial goals.

Adjust for Bonuses and Windfalls: If you receive a bonus, tax refund, or other windfall, consider increasing your automatic transfer amount temporarily to boost your savings.

Practical Example

Let's consider Mark, who wants to save for an emergency fund and a vacation. Mark decides to save $500 each month, with $300 going towards his emergency fund and $200 towards his vacation fund.

Choose the Right Savings Account: Mark opens two high-interest savings accounts, one for his emergency fund and another for his vacation fund.

Determine Savings Goals: His short-term goal is to save $3,600 for a vacation within 18 months, and his long-term goal is to build an emergency fund of $10,000.

Calculate How Much to Save: Mark decides to save a total of $500 per month.

Set Up Automatic Transfers: Mark logs into his online banking account and sets up two automatic transfers:

$300 from his checking account to his emergency fund savings account on the 1st of each month.

$200 from his checking account to his vacation fund savings account on the 15th of each month.

Monitor and Adjust: Every three months, Mark reviews his savings progress. If he receives a bonus at work, he adjusts his automatic transfers to temporarily increase the savings amounts.

Conclusion

Automatic savings is an effective strategy to ensure consistent and disciplined saving. By setting up automatic transfers to your savings accounts, you can simplify the process, prioritize your financial goals, and reduce the temptation to spend. Regularly reviewing and adjusting your automatic savings plan ensures it remains aligned with your financial situation and goals. This approach helps you build a robust financial foundation, paving the way for long-term financial stability and independence.

Chapter 4: Saving Strategies for Everyone

Finding Extra Savings

Tips for Cutting Expenses and Finding Savings in Daily Life

Finding extra savings in your daily life can significantly boost your ability to meet financial goals, whether you're building an emergency fund, saving for a major purchase, or simply trying to improve your overall financial health. Here are practical tips and strategies for cutting expenses and uncovering savings opportunities.

1. Track Your Spending

Expense Tracking Apps: Use apps like Mint, YNAB (You Need a Budget), or Personal Capital to track and categorize your spending. These tools provide a clear picture of where your money is going and help identify areas for potential savings.

Manual Tracking: Keep a spending diary or spreadsheet where you record all expenses. Reviewing this data regularly can reveal patterns and unnecessary expenditures.

2. Create and Stick to a Budget

Zero-Based Budgeting: Allocate every dollar of your income to a specific purpose, including savings, to ensure that all your money is accounted for.

Envelope System: Use physical or digital envelopes to set aside cash for different spending categories. Once an envelope is empty, stop spending in that category until the next budgeting period.

3. Reduce Discretionary Spending

Dining Out: Limit dining out to special occasions and cook more meals at home. Plan meals and make a shopping list to avoid impulse buys at the grocery store.

Entertainment: Look for free or low-cost entertainment options, such as community events, parks, or streaming services instead of expensive cable TV packages.

4. Save on Household Expenses

Energy Efficiency: Reduce utility bills by using energy-efficient appliances, insulating your home, and adopting habits like turning off lights and unplugging electronics when not in use.

Bulk Buying: Purchase non-perishable items in bulk to save money over time. Use warehouse memberships like Costco or Sam's Club, but only buy what you need to avoid waste.

5. Cut Transportation Costs

Public Transportation: Use public transit instead of driving. Many cities offer affordable monthly transit passes.

Carpooling: Share rides with colleagues or friends to reduce fuel and maintenance costs. Apps like Waze Carpool or Carpool World can help find carpool partners.

Biking or Walking: For short distances, consider biking or walking instead of driving. This not only saves money but also promotes a healthy lifestyle.

6. Evaluate Subscriptions and Memberships

Review Regularly: Periodically review all your subscriptions and memberships, such as streaming services, gym memberships, and magazine subscriptions. Cancel any that you don't use frequently.

Negotiate Lower Rates: Contact service providers to negotiate lower rates for internet, cable, and phone services. Mentioning competitor offers can often result in discounts.

7. Shop Smart

Use Coupons and Discounts: Take advantage of coupons, sales, and discount codes. Websites like RetailMeNot and Honey can help find the best deals.

Loyalty Programs: Join loyalty programs at stores you frequent to earn points, discounts, or cashback on your purchases.

Buy Generic: Opt for generic or store-brand products instead of name brands. They often have the same quality but at a lower price.

8. Save on Debt Repayment

Refinance Loans: If you have high-interest loans, consider refinancing to lower interest rates. This can reduce your monthly payments and total interest paid over time.

Debt Snowball/Avalanche Method: Use strategies like the debt snowball or avalanche method to pay off debt more efficiently. The snowball method focuses on paying off the smallest balances first, while the avalanche method targets the highest interest rate debts.

9. Maximize Employee Benefits

Retirement Contributions: Contribute to employer-sponsored retirement plans, especially if your employer offers matching contributions. This is essentially free money towards your retirement savings.

Flexible Spending Accounts (FSAs): Use FSAs to pay for medical and childcare expenses with pre-tax dollars, reducing your taxable income.

10. Find Additional Income Sources

Side Hustles: Explore side hustles or freelance work to supplement your income. Popular options include driving for ride-share services, freelance writing, or selling handmade items online.

Passive Income: Invest in opportunities that generate passive income, such as rental properties, dividend-paying stocks, or peer-to-peer lending platforms.

Practical Examples

Example 1: Reducing Monthly Grocery Bill

Meal Planning: Plan your meals for the week and create a shopping list based on your plan. Stick to the list to avoid impulse purchases.

Bulk Cooking: Prepare meals in bulk and freeze portions for later. This reduces the need for expensive takeout on busy days.

Discount Stores: Shop at discount grocery stores or farmers' markets to find lower prices on fresh produce and other essentials.

Example 2: Cutting Utility Costs

Energy Audit: Conduct a home energy audit to identify ways to reduce energy consumption. Many utility companies offer free or low-cost audits.

Programmable Thermostat: Install a programmable thermostat to automatically adjust the temperature when you're not home, saving on heating and cooling costs.

Water-Saving Fixtures: Use water-saving showerheads and faucets to reduce water consumption and lower your water bill.

Example 3: Saving on Transportation

Public Transit Pass: Purchase a monthly public transit pass instead of paying for individual rides. This is often cheaper if you use public transit regularly.

Bike to Work: Invest in a reliable bicycle and bike to work when possible. This saves money on fuel, parking, and car maintenance.

Example 4: Lowering Entertainment Expenses

Streaming Services: Replace cable TV with cheaper streaming services like Netflix, Hulu, or Disney+. Consider sharing subscriptions with family or friends.

Free Events: Look for free local events such as outdoor concerts, movie nights, and community festivals. Websites like Meetup and Eventbrite can help you find events.

Conclusion

Finding extra savings in your daily life involves being mindful of your spending habits and making small adjustments that can add up to significant savings over time. By tracking your expenses, creating a budget, and employing strategies to reduce discretionary spending, household costs, transportation expenses, and more, you can free up money to allocate towards your savings goals. These practical tips and examples provide a roadmap to help you uncover savings opportunities and build a stronger financial foundation.

Chapter 5: Managing Debt

1. Types of Debt

Understanding Good vs. Bad Debt

Debt can be a useful financial tool when managed correctly, but it's crucial to distinguish between good debt and bad debt. Understanding the differences helps you make informed decisions about borrowing and managing your finances effectively.

What is Good Debt?

Good debt is typically associated with borrowing that can enhance your financial position over time. This type of debt often involves investments in things that have the potential to increase in value or generate income.

Educational Loans

Investment in Human Capital: Student loans are considered good debt because they fund education, which can significantly increase your earning potential. Higher education levels often correlate with higher salaries and better job opportunities.

Low Interest Rates: Many student loans offer relatively low-interest rates and favorable repayment terms, making them a manageable form of debt.

Mortgages

Real Estate Investment: A mortgage is a loan used to purchase property, which typically appreciates over time. Homeownership builds equity, and owning property can be a long-term financial asset.

Tax Benefits: Mortgage interest payments can often be deducted from your taxable income, providing additional financial benefits.

Business Loans

Business Growth: Borrowing to start or expand a business can be considered good debt if it leads to business growth and increased profits. This type of debt is an investment in your entrepreneurial future.

Leverage: Using borrowed funds to finance business activities can leverage growth and expansion opportunities that might not be possible with your own capital alone.

Auto Loans (for Necessary Transportation)

Essential Asset: An auto loan can be good debt if it finances a vehicle that is essential for your daily life, particularly if the car is necessary for commuting to work or running a business.

Resale Value: While cars typically depreciate, maintaining a reliable vehicle can be a necessary expense. Opting for a reasonably priced, reliable car rather than a luxury model can make an auto loan more justifiable.

What is Bad Debt?

Bad debt is generally associated with borrowing for items that do not increase in value or generate income. This type of debt often involves high-interest rates and can lead to financial strain if not managed properly.

Credit Card Debt

High Interest Rates: Credit cards often carry very high-interest rates, making it easy to accumulate significant debt if not paid off monthly. Interest charges can quickly escalate, making repayment difficult.

Consumer Purchases: Using credit cards to finance everyday expenses or non-essential purchases can lead to accumulating debt on depreciating items or consumables.

Payday Loans

Extremely High Interest Rates: Payday loans are short-term loans with exorbitant interest rates and fees. They are intended for emergency situations but can trap borrowers in a cycle of debt.

Debt Cycle: Due to their high costs and short repayment terms, many borrowers find it challenging to repay payday loans on time, leading to repeated borrowing and escalating debt.

Auto Loans (for Luxury or Unnecessary Vehicles)

Depreciating Asset: While an auto loan can be good debt for a necessary vehicle, borrowing to buy a luxury or expensive car that depreciates quickly is considered bad debt. The car's value often drops faster than the loan balance decreases.

High Monthly Payments: High car payments can strain your budget and reduce your ability to save or invest in appreciating assets.

Personal Loans for Non-Essential Expenses

Lifestyle Inflation: Taking out personal loans for vacations, weddings, or luxury items can lead to debt that does not provide a return on investment. These expenses are often one-time events with no lasting financial benefits.

Interest Costs: Even if the interest rates on personal loans are lower than credit cards, the borrowed money for non-essential expenses can divert funds from savings or investment opportunities.

Practical Examples of Good vs. Bad Debt

Good Debt Example: Student Loan

Sarah takes out a student loan to pursue a degree in engineering. After graduating, she secures a well-paying job, enabling her to pay off the loan comfortably. Her higher salary provides a good return on her educational investment.

Bad Debt Example: Credit Card Debt

John uses his credit card to buy the latest smartphone and designer clothes. He only makes minimum payments each month, and the high-interest rate causes his debt to grow. These purchases do not increase in value, leaving him with significant debt and no financial gain.

Good Debt Example: Mortgage

Lisa and Mark buy a house with a mortgage. Over the years, the value of their home appreciates, and they build equity. The mortgage interest is tax-deductible, and the home serves as a long-term investment.

Bad Debt Example: Payday Loan

Tom takes out a payday loan to cover an unexpected expense. The loan has a high-interest rate, and he struggles to repay it by the due date, leading to additional fees and another payday loan. This cycle traps him in a growing debt burden.

Conclusion

Understanding the difference between good and bad debt is essential for effective financial management. Good debt can enhance your financial position and contribute to long-term wealth, while bad debt can hinder your financial progress and lead to significant stress. By prioritizing borrowing for investments that increase in value or generate income and avoiding high-interest loans for depreciating assets, you can use debt as a tool to achieve financial independence and stability.

Chapter 5: Managing Debt

Debt Repayment Strategies

Snowball vs. Avalanche Methods

Effectively managing and repaying debt is a crucial step towards achieving financial independence. Two popular debt repayment strategies are the snowball method and the avalanche method. Both approaches have their own advantages and can be tailored to fit your financial situation and personal preferences.

Snowball Method

The snowball method involves paying off your smallest debts first, regardless of interest rates. This strategy focuses on building momentum and motivation as you see debts being eliminated one by one.

How It Works

List Your Debts: Arrange your debts from the smallest balance to the largest balance.

Minimum Payments: Continue making minimum payments on all your debts.

Focus on the Smallest Debt: Direct any extra money you have towards paying off the smallest debt first.

Celebrate and Move On: Once the smallest debt is paid off, celebrate the win. Then, move on to the next smallest debt, applying the same strategy.

Repeat: Continue this process until all your debts are paid off.

Advantages

Quick Wins: Paying off small debts quickly provides a sense of accomplishment and keeps you motivated to continue.

Psychological Boost: Seeing progress can boost your confidence and encourage you to stick with your repayment plan.

Simplification: As you eliminate smaller debts, you have fewer accounts to manage, simplifying your financial situation.

Disadvantages

Interest Costs: Because this method doesn't prioritize high-interest debts, you might pay more in interest over time compared to other methods.

Longer Time for Large Debts: Larger debts with high balances may take longer to address, potentially prolonging your overall repayment period.

Avalanche Method

The avalanche method focuses on minimizing the amount of interest you pay by targeting debts with the highest interest rates first. This strategy is more cost-effective in the long run.

How It Works

List Your Debts: Arrange your debts from the highest interest rate to the lowest interest rate.

Minimum Payments: Continue making minimum payments on all your debts.

Focus on the Highest Interest Debt: Direct any extra money you have towards paying off the debt with the highest interest rate first.

Move On: Once the highest interest debt is paid off, move on to the next highest interest rate debt.

Repeat: Continue this process until all your debts are paid off.

Advantages

Interest Savings: By focusing on high-interest debts, you reduce the total amount of interest paid over the life of your debts.

Faster Debt Reduction: Reducing high-interest debts first can lead to faster overall debt reduction.

Financial Efficiency: This method is mathematically the most efficient way to pay down debt.

Disadvantages

Slow Progress: Paying off high-interest debts first may mean that you don't see debts being eliminated as quickly, which can be discouraging.

Motivation: Without the quick wins that the snowball method provides, it can be harder to stay motivated.

Choosing the Right Method

Choosing between the snowball and avalanche methods depends on your financial situation and personal preferences. Consider the following factors:

Motivation and Discipline: If you need quick wins to stay motivated, the snowball method might be better for you. If you are disciplined and focused on minimizing interest costs, the avalanche method is likely more suitable.

Financial Goals: If your primary goal is to reduce the total interest paid, the avalanche method is the best choice. If simplifying your financial situation quickly is more important, the snowball method may be preferable.

Debt Profile: Assess your debts to determine which strategy will have the greatest impact. If you have high-interest credit card debt, the avalanche method can save you a significant amount of money.

Practical Example

Let's consider Emma, who has the following debts:

Credit Card Debt: $1,000 at 20% interest

Car Loan: $5,000 at 7% interest

Student Loan: $10,000 at 5% interest

Personal Loan: $2,000 at 15% interest

Snowball Method:

Step 1: Pay off the credit card debt ($1,000) first while making minimum payments on other debts.

Step 2: Move to the personal loan ($2,000).

Step 3: Pay off the car loan ($5,000).

Step 4: Finally, tackle the student loan ($10,000).

Avalanche Method:

Step 1: Pay off the credit card debt ($1,000) first due to its 20% interest rate.

Step 2: Move to the personal loan ($2,000) with a 15% interest rate.

Step 3: Pay off the car loan ($5,000) with a 7% interest rate.

Step 4: Lastly, tackle the student loan ($10,000) with a 5% interest rate.

Combining Methods

Some people prefer a hybrid approach, combining elements of both methods. For example, starting with the snowball method to build momentum and then switching to the avalanche method to minimize interest costs once initial debts are cleared.

Conclusion

Both the snowball and avalanche methods offer effective strategies for debt repayment. The snowball method provides psychological motivation through quick wins, while the avalanche method focuses on minimizing interest costs and achieving financial efficiency. By understanding the advantages and disadvantages of each approach, you can choose the strategy that best aligns with your financial goals and personal preferences, paving the way for successful debt management and financial independence.

Chapter 5: Managing Debt

Avoiding Debt Traps

Tips for Staying Out of Unnecessary Debt

Avoiding debt traps is essential for maintaining financial health and achieving long-term financial goals. By adopting smart financial habits and making informed decisions, you can steer clear of unnecessary debt and build a solid foundation for financial stability. Here are practical tips to help you avoid common debt traps:

Create a Budget and Stick to It

Track Your Spending: Monitor your expenses regularly to understand where your money is going. Use budgeting apps or spreadsheets to categorize spending and identify areas where you can cut back.

Set Realistic Goals: Establish clear financial goals and prioritize your spending accordingly. Allocate funds towards essentials like housing, utilities, groceries, and savings before discretionary expenses.

Build an Emergency Fund

Prepare for the Unexpected: Having an emergency fund provides a financial safety net to cover unexpected expenses like medical emergencies, car repairs, or job loss. Aim to save three to six months' worth of living expenses in a dedicated savings account.

Avoid Impulse Purchases

Practice Delayed Gratification: Before making a purchase, especially for non-essential items, give yourself time to consider whether it's a necessity or a want. Avoid impulse buys by waiting at least 24 hours before making a decision.

Stick to Shopping Lists: Make shopping lists before going to the grocery store or running errands and stick to them. Avoid browsing aisles or websites where you're likely to be tempted by unnecessary items.

Live Below Your Means

Spend Less Than You Earn: Strive to live below your means by spending less than you earn. Avoid lifestyle inflation that comes with increasing your spending as your income rises.

Practice Frugality: Look for ways to save money on everyday expenses without sacrificing quality of life. Consider buying used items, shopping for discounts, or negotiating lower bills.

Use Credit Wisely

Limit Credit Card Usage: Use credit cards responsibly and avoid carrying balances from month to month. Pay off your credit card balances in full to avoid high-interest charges.

Understand Loan Terms: Before taking out any loans, understand the terms and conditions, including interest rates, fees, and repayment schedules. Avoid payday loans and other high-cost forms of credit whenever possible.

Prioritize High-Interest Debt

Focus on Debt Repayment: If you have existing debt, prioritize paying off high-interest debt first to minimize interest costs. Consider using debt repayment strategies like the avalanche method to tackle debts strategically.

Avoid Minimum Payments: Pay more than the minimum payment on your debts whenever possible. Making only minimum payments prolongs the repayment period and increases the total interest paid.

Seek Financial Education

Increase Financial Literacy: Educate yourself about personal finance topics, including budgeting, saving, investing, and debt management. Take advantage of free resources like books, websites, podcasts, and financial workshops.

Consult Financial Professionals: If you're unsure about financial decisions or need personalized advice, consider consulting with a financial advisor or counselor. They can provide guidance tailored to your specific circumstances and goals.

Plan for Major Expenses

Anticipate Large Costs: Plan ahead for major expenses like home repairs, car maintenance, or medical bills by setting aside funds in advance. Establish sinking funds or designated savings accounts for these purposes.

Avoid Lifestyle Creep: Be cautious about increasing your spending in anticipation of windfalls like bonuses or tax refunds. Instead, allocate these funds towards savings goals or debt repayment.

Stay Mindful of Peer Pressure

Resist Social Influences: Don't succumb to peer pressure or societal norms that promote excessive spending or lifestyle inflation. Focus on your own financial priorities and values rather than trying to keep up with others.

Surround Yourself with Supportive Peers: Surround yourself with friends and family who understand and respect your financial goals. Seek out like-minded individuals who prioritize financial responsibility and frugality.

Regularly Review and Adjust

Monitor Your Financial Progress: Regularly review your financial situation, including your budget, savings, debt balances, and financial goals. Make adjustments as needed to stay on track and address any challenges that arise.

Celebrate Milestones: Celebrate your financial achievements and milestones along the way, whether it's paying off a debt, reaching a savings goal, or sticking to your budget. Recognize your progress and use it as motivation to continue your financial journey.

Conclusion

Avoiding debt traps requires discipline, financial literacy, and smart decision-making. By following these tips for staying out of unnecessary debt, you can build a solid financial foundation, reduce financial stress, and work towards achieving your long-term financial goals. Whether it's creating a budget, practicing frugality, using credit wisely, or seeking financial education, each step you take towards responsible financial management brings you closer to financial independence and peace of mind.

Chapter 6: Income Enhancement

1. Multiple Income Streams

Importance of Diversifying Income Sources

Diversifying your income sources is a key strategy for achieving financial independence and stability. Relying on a single income stream can be risky, especially in today's volatile job market and economy. By developing multiple income streams, you can protect yourself against financial disruptions, increase your earning potential, and accelerate your journey toward financial independence.

Benefits of Multiple Income Streams

Financial Security

Risk Mitigation: If you lose one source of income due to job loss, economic downturns, or unforeseen circumstances, other income streams can help you maintain financial stability and cover your expenses.

Steady Cash Flow: Multiple income streams ensure a more consistent and reliable cash flow. This stability can help you manage monthly expenses, build savings, and invest for the future.

Increased Earning Potential

Supplemental Income: Additional income streams can supplement your primary income, allowing you to earn more money and achieve financial goals faster.

Income Growth: Diversifying your income sources can lead to exponential growth in your overall income, as you tap into different markets and opportunities.

Personal and Professional Development

Skill Diversification: Engaging in various income-generating activities can help you develop new skills, broaden your expertise, and enhance your employability.

Entrepreneurial Experience: Creating and managing different income streams can provide valuable entrepreneurial experience and foster innovation and creativity.

Retirement Preparation

Passive Income: Building multiple income streams, especially passive income sources, can provide financial support during retirement. This can reduce your reliance on retirement savings and social security benefits.

Long-Term Wealth: Diversifying income streams can help you accumulate wealth over time, ensuring a more comfortable and secure retirement.

Types of Income Streams

Active Income

Primary Job: Your main source of income, typically a full-time job or primary occupation.

Side Hustles: Part-time jobs or freelance work that provide additional income. Examples include consulting, tutoring, or gig economy jobs like driving for a ride-sharing service.

Passive Income

Investments: Income generated from dividends, interest, or capital gains from stocks, bonds, mutual funds, or real estate.

Rental Income: Earnings from renting out properties, whether residential, commercial, or vacation rentals.

Royalties: Income from intellectual property such as books, music, patents, or software licenses.

Online Businesses: Earnings from e-commerce stores, affiliate marketing, or digital products like courses or e-books.

Portfolio Income

Dividend Stocks: Investing in dividend-paying stocks that provide regular income distributions.

Real Estate Investment Trusts (REITs): Investments in REITs can generate income from real estate properties without the need to manage them directly.

Peer-to-Peer Lending: Participating in P2P lending platforms where you earn interest by lending money to individuals or small businesses.

Strategies for Building Multiple Income Streams

Leverage Your Skills and Interests

Identify Talents: Assess your skills, talents, and hobbies that can be monetized. For example, if you are skilled in graphic design, consider freelancing or selling design templates online.

Continuous Learning: Invest in education and training to acquire new skills that can open up additional income opportunities.

Start Small and Scale Up

Begin with Side Hustles: Start with manageable side hustles that fit your schedule and gradually expand as you gain experience and confidence.

Reinvest Earnings: Use earnings from side hustles or passive income streams to reinvest in growing these ventures or creating new ones.

Utilize Technology

Online Platforms: Take advantage of online platforms and marketplaces to reach a broader audience and generate income. Examples include selling products on Etsy, offering services on Fiverr, or creating a YouTube channel.

Automation Tools: Use automation tools and software to streamline and manage multiple income streams efficiently. This can help you save time and focus on scaling your efforts.

Network and Collaborate

Join Communities: Engage with communities and networks in your areas of interest to learn from others, share ideas, and find collaboration opportunities.

Partnerships: Consider forming partnerships or joint ventures with like-minded individuals or businesses to create new income streams and share resources.

Case Study: Sarah's Multiple Income Streams

Sarah, a marketing professional, wanted to achieve financial independence and diversify her income. Here's how she created multiple income streams:

Primary Job: Sarah continued working full-time as a marketing manager, providing her primary source of income and benefits.

Freelance Work: She started offering freelance marketing services to small businesses, leveraging her expertise and earning extra income.

Online Courses: Sarah created online marketing courses and sold them on platforms like Udemy and Teachable, generating passive income.

Dividend Investments: She invested in dividend-paying stocks and reinvested the dividends to grow her portfolio.

Real Estate: Sarah purchased a rental property, generating monthly rental income and building equity over time.

E-Book: She wrote an e-book on marketing strategies for small businesses and sold it on Amazon Kindle, earning royalties.

By diversifying her income sources, Sarah achieved greater financial security, increased her earning potential, and moved closer to financial independence.

Conclusion

Diversifying your income sources is a powerful strategy for enhancing financial security and achieving financial independence. By creating multiple income streams, you can mitigate risks, increase your earning potential, and build long-term wealth. Whether through active income, passive income, or portfolio income, exploring and developing various income opportunities can provide you with financial stability and freedom. Start small, leverage your skills, utilize technology, and continuously seek new opportunities to create a robust and resilient financial future.

Chapter 6: Income Enhancement

2. Side Hustles

Ideas and Tips for Starting Side Hustles

Side hustles are additional jobs or projects that you take on outside of your primary employment to earn extra income. They can provide financial stability, help you pay off debt faster, and enable you to save or invest more money. Here are some practical ideas and tips for starting side hustles that can enhance your income.

Popular Side Hustle Ideas

Freelancing

Writing and Editing: Offer your services as a freelance writer, editor, or proofreader. Platforms like Upwork, Freelancer, and Fiverr connect freelancers with clients looking for various writing-related services.

Graphic Design: Use your design skills to create logos, business cards, and marketing materials for clients. Websites like 99designs and Behance can showcase your portfolio and attract potential clients.

Web Development: Provide web development and design services for small businesses or individuals. Use platforms like Toptal and Guru to find clients.

Tutoring and Teaching

Academic Tutoring: Offer tutoring services in subjects you excel at. You can do this locally or online through platforms like Tutor.com, Wyzant, or Chegg Tutors.

Language Teaching: Teach a language you are fluent in through platforms like iTalki or VIPKid, which connect tutors with students worldwide.

Online Courses: Create and sell online courses on platforms like Udemy, Coursera, or Teachable. Share your knowledge in areas such as business, technology, arts, or personal development.

Gig Economy Jobs

Ridesharing: Drive for companies like Uber or Lyft to earn extra income by providing transportation services.

Delivery Services: Deliver food, groceries, or packages through services like DoorDash, Postmates, Instacart, or Amazon Flex.

Task Services: Offer your skills for various tasks and errands through platforms like TaskRabbit.

Creative Endeavors

Handmade Crafts: Sell handmade items such as jewelry, clothing, or home decor on platforms like Etsy.

Photography: Offer photography services for events, portraits, or stock photos. Sell your photos on stock photography websites like Shutterstock or Adobe Stock.

Music and Art: Create and sell your music or artwork. Platforms like Bandcamp and ArtStation can help you reach a broader audience.

Real Estate and Rental Services

Rent Out Property: Rent out a room, apartment, or house on platforms like Airbnb or VRBO.

Car Rental: Rent out your car when you're not using it through services like Turo.

Online and E-Commerce Businesses

Dropshipping: Start a dropshipping business where you sell products without holding inventory. Use platforms like Shopify to set up your online store.

Affiliate Marketing: Promote products or services and earn a commission for each sale made through your referral links. Join affiliate programs from companies like Amazon Associates or ShareASale.

Print on Demand: Create and sell custom-designed products like T-shirts, mugs, or phone cases through print-on-demand services like Printful or Redbubble.

Tips for Starting a Successful Side Hustle

Identify Your Skills and Interests

Leverage Your Strengths: Choose side hustles that align with your skills, expertise, and interests. This increases your chances of success and enjoyment.

Passion Projects: Consider side hustles that you are passionate about. When you enjoy what you do, it won't feel like extra work.

Start Small and Scale Gradually

Test the Waters: Start with a small project or limited hours to gauge interest and feasibility. Gradually expand as you gain confidence and experience.

Manage Your Time: Balance your side hustle with your primary job and personal life. Create a schedule that allows you to dedicate time to your side hustle without burnout.

Utilize Online Platforms

Marketplaces and Freelance Websites: Use established platforms to find clients and customers. These platforms provide visibility and credibility, making it easier to get started.

Social Media and Networking: Promote your side hustle on social media and network with potential clients or collaborators. Building an online presence can help attract more business.

Offer Quality Services and Products

Deliver Excellence: Provide high-quality services or products to build a good reputation and gain repeat business. Satisfied customers are likely to refer you to others.

Seek Feedback: Continuously seek feedback from your clients or customers to improve your offerings and meet their needs better.

Manage Finances Wisely

Separate Accounts: Keep your side hustle income and expenses separate from your personal finances. This helps with budgeting, tracking profits, and managing taxes.

Invest Earnings: Reinvest a portion of your earnings back into your side hustle to grow your business. Whether it's marketing, equipment, or education, reinvesting can help you scale faster.

Stay Compliant with Regulations

Understand Legal Requirements: Ensure you comply with local laws and regulations related to your side hustle. This includes business licenses, tax obligations, and any industry-specific rules.

Insurance: Consider obtaining insurance if your side hustle involves risks, such as liability insurance for freelancers or property insurance for rental services.

Case Study: Jake's Side Hustle Journey

Jake, a software engineer, wanted to diversify his income and explore his passion for photography. Here's how he successfully started and grew his side hustles:

Freelance Coding: Jake began offering freelance coding services on Upwork, focusing on small projects that fit his schedule. He used his existing skills to earn additional income without much initial investment.

Stock Photography: Jake turned his photography hobby into a side hustle by selling his photos on stock photography websites like Shutterstock and Adobe Stock. This passive income stream grew as he uploaded more high-quality images.

Online Courses: Leveraging his expertise in software development, Jake created an online course on web development and sold it on Udemy. This provided a significant boost to his income through course sales and royalties.

By balancing his primary job with these side hustles, Jake was able to increase his income, pay off debt, and save for future goals.

Conclusion

Starting a side hustle can be a rewarding way to enhance your income and achieve financial independence. Whether you choose freelancing, teaching, gig economy jobs, creative endeavors, real estate, or e-commerce, there are countless opportunities to explore. By identifying your skills, starting small, utilizing online platforms, offering quality services, managing finances wisely, and staying compliant with regulations, you can successfully build and grow your side hustle. Embrace the entrepreneurial spirit, and take proactive steps to diversify your income streams and secure your financial future.

Chapter 6: Income Enhancement

Maximizing Earnings

Negotiation Tips for Higher Salaries or Rates

Maximizing your earnings through effective negotiation can significantly impact your financial independence journey. Whether you're negotiating a higher salary at your current job, seeking a raise, or setting rates for freelance work, mastering negotiation skills is crucial. Here are detailed tips and strategies to help you negotiate higher salaries or rates successfully.

1. Prepare Thoroughly

Research Market Rates: Understand the market rates for your role, industry, and geographic location. Websites like Glassdoor, Payscale, and LinkedIn Salary Insights provide valuable data on salary ranges and compensation packages.

Know Your Value: Assess your skills, experience, and achievements. Prepare a list of your accomplishments, highlighting how you have contributed to your organization or clients. Quantify your achievements with metrics, such as revenue generated, cost savings, or projects completed.

2. Build a Strong Case

Document Your Achievements: Create a portfolio or presentation that showcases your work, including key projects, client testimonials, and performance reviews. This evidence can strengthen your case during negotiations.

Highlight Unique Skills: Emphasize any unique skills or expertise that set you apart from others in your field. Specialized knowledge, certifications, or advanced degrees can justify a higher salary or rate.

3. Timing Matters

Choose the Right Moment: Time your negotiation strategically. For salary negotiations, consider times when the company is performing well, during performance reviews, or when you have recently completed a successful project. For freelancers, negotiate rates at the beginning of a project or after demonstrating your value through initial work.

Leverage Offers: If you have received job offers from other companies, use them as leverage. Politely inform your current employer about the offer and express your interest in staying if they can match or exceed the competing offer.

4. Communicate Effectively

Be Confident and Assertive: Approach the negotiation with confidence and assertiveness. Clearly state your desired salary or rate and the reasons why you believe you deserve it.

Practice Active Listening: Listen to the other party's concerns and objections. Understand their perspective and address their points with well-reasoned arguments.

Stay Professional: Maintain a professional tone throughout the negotiation. Avoid being confrontational or aggressive. Focus on a collaborative approach, aiming for a win-win outcome.

5. Negotiate Beyond Salary

Consider Total Compensation: Look beyond the base salary or hourly rate. Negotiate for additional benefits such as bonuses, stock options, health insurance, retirement contributions, flexible working hours, professional development opportunities, and additional paid time off.

Tailor Your Requests: Customize your negotiation requests based on your needs and priorities. For example, if work-life balance is important to you, emphasize flexible working arrangements or remote work options.

6. Practice Negotiation Skills

Role-Playing: Practice your negotiation skills with a friend or mentor. Role-playing different scenarios can help you anticipate questions, refine your responses, and build confidence.

Seek Feedback: After each negotiation, reflect on what went well and areas for improvement. Seek feedback from trusted colleagues or mentors to enhance your negotiation techniques.

7. Be Prepared to Walk Away

Know Your Worth: If your employer or client is unwilling to meet your reasonable salary or rate expectations, be prepared to walk away. Knowing your worth and having confidence in your value can give you the strength to seek better opportunities elsewhere.

Have a Backup Plan: Always have a backup plan in place. This could be another job offer, a list of potential clients, or savings to support you during the transition.

Case Study: Emma's Successful Salary Negotiation

Emma, a marketing manager with five years of experience, decided to negotiate her salary after consistently exceeding performance targets. Here's how she approached the negotiation:

Preparation: Emma researched the market rates for marketing managers in her city and industry. She found that her salary was below the average range for her role and experience level.

Building a Case: Emma documented her achievements, including a 20% increase in social media engagement and a successful product launch that generated significant revenue. She prepared a presentation highlighting these accomplishments.

Timing: Emma chose to negotiate during her annual performance review, a time when her contributions were fresh in her employer's mind.

Effective Communication: Emma confidently presented her case, stating her desired salary increase and backing it up with her research and documented achievements. She also expressed her commitment to the company and her desire to continue contributing to its success.

Total Compensation: In addition to a higher base salary, Emma negotiated for additional vacation days and a professional development stipend.

Outcome: Emma's employer recognized her value and agreed to a 15% salary increase, additional vacation days, and a yearly stipend for professional development.

Conclusion

Negotiating higher salaries or rates is a critical skill that can significantly enhance your income and accelerate your path to financial independence. By preparing thoroughly, building a strong case, choosing the right timing, communicating effectively, considering total compensation, practicing your skills, and being prepared to walk away, you can successfully maximize your earnings. Approach each negotiation with confidence, professionalism, and a clear understanding of your value to achieve the best possible outcome.

Chapter 7: Basics of Investing

1. Why Invest?

Importance of Investing for Long-Term Wealth

Investing is a fundamental strategy for building long-term wealth and achieving financial independence. By putting your money to work through various investment vehicles, you can grow your wealth over time, outpace inflation, and create financial security for the future. Here's an in-depth look at why investing is crucial and the benefits it offers.

1. Building Wealth Over Time

Compound Interest: One of the most powerful concepts in investing is compound interest, which means earning interest on your initial investment as well as on the interest that accumulates over time. The longer you invest, the more your money can grow exponentially. For example, if you invest $1,000 at an annual return of 7%, it will grow to $1,967 in 10 years, $3,870 in 20 years, and $7,612 in 30 years, without any additional contributions.

Capital Appreciation: Investments like stocks, real estate, and mutual funds can appreciate in value over time, significantly increasing your wealth. For instance, investing in a well-diversified stock portfolio can yield substantial returns as companies grow and their stock prices rise.

2. Outpacing Inflation

Maintaining Purchasing Power: Inflation erodes the purchasing power of money over time. What you can buy with $100 today will cost more in the future due to rising prices. Investing in assets that typically outpace inflation, such as stocks and real estate, helps preserve and increase your purchasing power.

Real Returns: While savings accounts and fixed deposits provide nominal returns, these often do not keep pace with inflation. By investing in higher-yielding assets, you can achieve real returns that grow your wealth beyond the inflation rate.

3. Diversification and Risk Management

Spreading Risk: Investing allows you to diversify your portfolio across different asset classes, such as stocks, bonds, real estate, and commodities. Diversification reduces the risk of significant losses because the performance of different investments is not perfectly correlated.

Risk and Reward Balance: Different investments carry varying levels of risk and potential reward. By balancing high-risk, high-reward investments with low-risk, stable investments, you can optimize your risk-reward ratio according to your financial goals and risk tolerance.

4. Achieving Financial Goals

Short-Term Goals: Investing can help you achieve short-term financial goals, such as saving for a down payment on a house, a new car, or a vacation. Short-term investments might include high-yield savings accounts, certificates of deposit (CDs), or short-term bonds.

Long-Term Goals: For long-term goals like retirement, education funding for children, or building a legacy, investing in growth-oriented assets like stocks, real estate, and mutual funds can provide the necessary returns to meet these objectives.

5. Retirement Planning

Building a Retirement Nest Egg: Investing is essential for building a retirement nest egg that can support you in your later years. Pension plans, 401(k)s, IRAs, and other retirement accounts allow your investments to grow tax-deferred or tax-free, depending on the account type.

Income Generation: Investments such as dividend-paying stocks, rental properties, and bonds can provide a steady income stream during retirement, supplementing other sources of retirement income like social security or pensions.

6. Financial Independence and Early Retirement (FIRE)

Achieving FIRE: The Financial Independence, Retire Early (FIRE) movement emphasizes aggressive saving and investing to achieve financial independence and retire early. By consistently investing a significant portion of your income and living below your means, you can build a substantial investment portfolio that generates enough passive income to cover your living expenses.

Freedom and Flexibility: Achieving financial independence through investing provides the freedom to pursue your passions, travel, volunteer, or start a business without being tied to a traditional 9-to-5 job.

Case Study: The Power of Long-Term Investing

Consider Sarah, who starts investing $5,000 annually at the age of 25 in a diversified stock portfolio with an average annual return of 7%. By the time she reaches 65, her investment would have grown to approximately $1,035,000. If Sarah had waited until she was 35 to start investing, she would only have around $505,000 by age 65, assuming the same annual contributions and returns. This example illustrates the significant impact of starting early and the power of compounding over time.

Conclusion

Investing is a crucial component of building long-term wealth and achieving financial goals. By leveraging the power of compound interest, outpacing inflation, diversifying risks, and aligning investments with both short-term and long-term goals, you can create a robust financial future. Whether planning for retirement, pursuing financial independence, or securing your family's future, investing wisely is essential to growing your wealth and achieving financial stability. Start investing early, remain consistent, and focus on long-term growth to maximize your financial potential.

Chapter 7: Basics of Investing

Types of Investments

Investing offers a variety of options, each with its own characteristics, benefits, and risks. Understanding the different types of investments can help you build a diversified portfolio that aligns with your financial goals and risk tolerance. Here are some of the most common types of investments: stocks, bonds, real estate, mutual funds, and exchange-traded funds (ETFs).

1. Stocks

Definition: Stocks represent ownership shares in a company. When you buy a stock, you become a partial owner of that company.

Benefits:

Potential for High Returns: Historically, stocks have provided higher returns than most other asset classes over the long term.

Dividends: Some companies pay dividends, providing a regular income stream in addition to potential capital gains.

Risks:

Volatility: Stock prices can fluctuate significantly in the short term due to market conditions, company performance, and economic factors.

Market Risk: Stocks are subject to market risk, where the overall market trends affect individual stock prices.

2. Bonds

Definition: Bonds are debt securities issued by governments, municipalities, or corporations to raise capital. When you buy a bond, you are lending money to the issuer in exchange for periodic interest payments and the return of the bond's face value at maturity.

Benefits:

Steady Income: Bonds provide regular interest payments, making them a reliable income source.

Lower Risk: Generally, bonds are considered less risky than stocks, especially government and high-quality corporate bonds.

Risks:

Interest Rate Risk: Bond prices inversely react to changes in interest rates. When rates rise, bond prices fall, and vice versa.

Credit Risk: There's a risk that the bond issuer might default on interest payments or fail to return the principal amount.

3. Real Estate

Definition: Real estate investing involves purchasing property, such as residential, commercial, or industrial real estate, to generate income or for capital appreciation.

Benefits:

Income Generation: Real estate can provide rental income.

Appreciation: Property values can increase over time, providing capital gains upon sale.

Diversification: Real estate often behaves differently from stocks and bonds, offering portfolio diversification.

Risks:

Liquidity Risk: Real estate is not as liquid as stocks or bonds; selling a property can take time and incur significant costs.

Market Risk: Real estate values can fluctuate based on market conditions, location, and economic factors.

4. Mutual Funds

Definition: Mutual funds pool money from many investors to buy a diversified portfolio of stocks, bonds, or other securities, managed by professional fund managers.

Benefits:

Diversification: Mutual funds offer instant diversification across many securities, reducing individual investment risk.

Professional Management: Funds are managed by experienced professionals who make investment decisions on behalf of investors.

Risks:

Management Fees: Mutual funds charge management fees, which can eat into returns.

Market Risk: The value of mutual funds can fluctuate based on the performance of the underlying assets.

5. Exchange-Traded Funds (ETFs)

Definition: ETFs are similar to mutual funds in that they hold a diversified portfolio of securities. However, they trade on stock exchanges like individual stocks.

Benefits:

Flexibility: ETFs can be bought and sold throughout the trading day at market prices, providing liquidity and flexibility.

Low Fees: ETFs generally have lower expense ratios compared to mutual funds.

Diversification: ETFs offer exposure to a broad range of assets, sectors, or markets, depending on their focus.

Risks:

Market Risk: ETFs are subject to market fluctuations based on the performance of the underlying assets.

Trading Costs: While ETFs have lower management fees, frequent trading can result in brokerage commissions and other costs.

Case Study: Diversified Portfolio Example

Consider John, who wants to build a diversified investment portfolio. Here's how he allocates his investments:

Stocks (40%): John invests in a mix of large-cap, mid-cap, and small-cap stocks across various industries. He focuses on both growth and dividend-paying stocks to balance potential capital appreciation and income.

Bonds (30%): He includes a variety of government and high-quality corporate bonds to provide stability and steady income.

Real Estate (15%): John invests in a real estate investment trust (REIT) to gain exposure to the real estate market without directly managing properties.

Mutual Funds (10%): He chooses a balanced mutual fund that holds a mix of stocks and bonds, benefiting from professional management and diversification.

ETFs (5%): John adds an ETF that tracks the S&P 500 index, providing broad market exposure with low fees.

By diversifying across different types of investments, John aims to achieve a balanced portfolio that can weather market fluctuations and provide long-term growth.

Conclusion

Understanding the different types of investments is essential for building a diversified and resilient portfolio. Stocks, bonds, real estate, mutual funds, and ETFs each offer unique benefits and risks. By combining these asset classes, you can create a balanced investment strategy that aligns with your financial goals, risk tolerance, and time horizon. Diversification not only helps manage risk but also provides opportunities for growth, income, and long-term wealth accumulation.

Chapter 7: Basics of Investing

Starting Small

How to Begin Investing with Limited Funds

Starting your investment journey can seem daunting, especially if you have limited funds. However, it's entirely possible to build a robust investment portfolio even with small amounts of money. Here's a detailed guide on how to begin investing with limited funds.

1. Understand the Power of Small Investments

Compound Interest: Even small investments can grow significantly over time thanks to the power of compound interest. The key is to start early and invest consistently.

Habit Formation: Investing small amounts regularly can help you develop a disciplined approach to saving and investing.

2. Set Clear Financial Goals

Short-Term and Long-Term Goals: Define what you want to achieve with your investments. Are you saving for a down payment on a house, building an emergency fund, or planning for retirement?

SMART Goals: Set Specific, Measurable, Achievable, Relevant, and Time-bound goals to guide your investment strategy.

3. Start with a Budget

Assess Your Finances: Review your income, expenses, debts, and savings to determine how much you can allocate for investing each month.

Cut Unnecessary Expenses: Identify areas where you can reduce spending to free up more money for investments.

4. Use Micro-Investing Apps

Round-Up Apps: Apps like Acorns and Qapital round up your everyday purchases to the nearest dollar and invest the spare change. This allows you to start investing with just a few dollars.

Fractional Shares: Platforms like Robinhood, Stash, and Betterment allow you to buy fractional shares of stocks and ETFs, meaning you can invest in high-value stocks with as little as $1.

5. Take Advantage of Employer-Sponsored Plans

401(k) or 403(b) Plans: If your employer offers a retirement plan, start contributing to it. Many employers match contributions up to a certain percentage, which is essentially free money.

Automatic Contributions: Set up automatic contributions to your retirement account to ensure consistent investing.

6. Open a Roth IRA or Traditional IRA

Tax-Advantaged Accounts: Individual Retirement Accounts (IRAs) offer tax advantages that can help your investments grow faster. Roth IRAs provide tax-free growth and withdrawals in retirement, while Traditional IRAs offer tax-deferred growth.

Low Minimums: Many financial institutions allow you to open an IRA with a low initial deposit and make small, regular contributions.

7. Invest in Low-Cost Index Funds and ETFs

Diversification: Index funds and ETFs provide broad market exposure, reducing the risk associated with individual stocks.

Low Fees: These funds typically have lower fees compared to actively managed funds, allowing more of your money to be invested.

8. Utilize Robo-Advisors

Automated Investing: Robo-advisors like Betterment, Wealthfront, and Ellevest use algorithms to create and manage a diversified portfolio based on your risk tolerance and goals.

Low Minimums: Many robo-advisors have low or no minimum investment requirements, making them accessible for new investors.

9. Educate Yourself

Learn the Basics: Read books, take online courses, and follow financial blogs to build your investment knowledge.

Stay Informed: Keep up with market trends and economic news to make informed investment decisions.

10. Start a High-Yield Savings Account

Emergency Fund: Before you start investing, ensure you have an emergency fund to cover unexpected expenses. A high-yield savings account can provide a safe place to store this money while earning interest.

Case Study: Starting Small and Growing Over Time

Consider Alex, who wants to start investing but only has $50 a month to spare. Here's how Alex can begin:

Budgeting: Alex reviews his finances and cuts back on non-essential expenses, freeing up $50 each month for investing.

Micro-Investing: He signs up for an app like Acorns, which rounds up his everyday purchases and invests the spare change. Over time, these small amounts add up.

Robo-Advisor: Alex also opens an account with a robo-advisor, investing his $50 monthly contribution into a diversified portfolio.

Employer Plan: Alex's employer offers a 401(k) with a matching contribution. He contributes enough to get the full match, ensuring he takes advantage of the free money.

Learning and Adjusting: Alex continuously educates himself about investing. As his income increases, he gradually increases his monthly investment contributions.

Conclusion

Starting small is an effective way to begin your investment journey. By leveraging micro-investing apps, employer-sponsored retirement plans, low-cost index funds, and robo-advisors, you can start building your wealth with limited funds. Consistency, education, and a disciplined approach are key to growing your investments over time. Remember, the most important step is to start investing early and regularly, no matter how small the initial amount may be.

Chapter 8: Long-Term Financial Planning

1. Retirement Planning

Importance of Planning for Retirement Early

Retirement planning is a critical aspect of long-term financial security. Starting early offers numerous advantages that can significantly impact your quality of life during retirement. Here's a detailed exploration of why early retirement planning is essential and how it benefits your financial future.

1. Maximizing Compound Interest

The Power of Compounding: The earlier you start saving for retirement, the more time your investments have to grow. Compound interest means you earn interest on your initial investment and on the interest that accumulates over time. This exponential growth can substantially increase your retirement savings.

Example: Consider two individuals, Jane and John. Jane starts saving $200 a month at age 25, while John starts saving $200 a month at age 35. Assuming an average annual return of 7%, Jane will have approximately $487,000 by age 65, whereas John will have around $227,000. Starting 10 years earlier allows Jane to accumulate more than double the amount, despite contributing the same monthly amount.

2. Reducing Financial Stress

Peace of Mind: Early retirement planning reduces financial anxiety and stress. Knowing that you are steadily building a retirement nest egg provides a sense of security and peace of mind.

Avoiding Last-Minute Rush: By starting early, you avoid the pressure of having to save large amounts of money closer to retirement age. This gradual approach is less stressful and more manageable.

3. Taking Advantage of Employer-Sponsored Plans

401(k) and 403(b) Plans: Many employers offer retirement plans such as 401(k)s or 403(b)s. Contributing to these plans early in your career can significantly boost your retirement savings, especially if your employer offers matching contributions.

Employer Matching: Employer matching contributions are essentially free money. By contributing enough to get the full match, you can maximize your retirement savings. Starting early ensures you take full advantage of this benefit over your entire career.

4. Tax Benefits

Tax-Deferred Growth: Retirement accounts such as Traditional IRAs and 401(k)s offer tax-deferred growth. This means you don't pay taxes on your investment gains until you withdraw the money in retirement, allowing your investments to grow faster.

Tax-Free Withdrawals: Roth IRAs provide tax-free growth and withdrawals in retirement, assuming you meet certain conditions. Starting early allows you to contribute to these accounts over a longer period, maximizing your tax-free savings.

5. Flexibility and Freedom

Early Retirement Options: Starting your retirement planning early gives you the flexibility to retire early if you choose. Achieving financial independence sooner allows you to make life choices based on your preferences rather than financial necessity.

Pursuing Passions: With adequate retirement savings, you have the freedom to pursue hobbies, travel, volunteer, or start a new career or business after retirement without financial constraints.

6. Mitigating Inflation

Preserving Purchasing Power: Over time, inflation erodes the purchasing power of money. By investing in assets that historically outpace inflation, such as stocks and real estate, you can preserve and grow your retirement savings.

Long-Term Growth: Starting early allows your investments to grow over several decades, helping to counteract the impact of inflation and ensuring you maintain your standard of living in retirement.

7. Adapting to Life Changes

Flexibility to Adjust: Life is unpredictable, and early retirement planning gives you the flexibility to adapt to changes such as career shifts, health issues, or family needs without compromising your retirement goals.

Buffer Against Uncertainty: Building a substantial retirement fund early provides a financial buffer that can protect you against unforeseen circumstances and emergencies.

Steps to Start Early Retirement Planning

Set Clear Goals: Define what you want your retirement to look like. Consider factors such as desired retirement age, lifestyle, travel plans, and expected living expenses.

Create a Retirement Plan: Develop a detailed retirement plan outlining your savings goals, investment strategy, and timeline. Use retirement calculators to estimate how much you need to save to achieve your goals.

Maximize Contributions: Take full advantage of retirement accounts like 401(k)s, IRAs, and Roth IRAs. Contribute the maximum amount allowed by law to benefit from tax advantages and compound growth.

Diversify Investments: Build a diversified investment portfolio that includes stocks, bonds, real estate, and other assets to spread risk and enhance growth potential.

Monitor and Adjust: Regularly review your retirement plan and investments. Adjust your strategy as needed based on changes in your financial situation, market conditions, and retirement goals.

Seek Professional Advice: Consider consulting a financial advisor to help you create and maintain a robust retirement plan tailored to your specific needs and goals.

Conclusion

Planning for retirement early is one of the most impactful financial decisions you can make. By starting early, you maximize the benefits of compound interest, reduce financial stress, take full advantage of employer-sponsored plans and tax benefits, and gain the flexibility and freedom to retire on your terms. Early planning also helps you mitigate inflation's impact, adapt to life changes, and build a secure financial future. Begin your retirement planning today to ensure a comfortable and fulfilling retirement.

Chapter 8: Long-Term Financial Planning

2. Retirement Accounts

Overview of Retirement Accounts from Different Countries

Retirement accounts vary significantly across countries, each with unique policies, tax advantages, and contribution limits. Understanding these differences is essential for effective long-term financial planning. This section provides an overview of retirement accounts in several countries, highlighting their distinct features and benefits.

1. United States

401(k) Plans:

Overview: Employer-sponsored retirement savings plans allowing employees to contribute a portion of their salary before taxes.

Tax Benefits: Contributions are tax-deferred, and taxes are paid upon withdrawal in retirement.

Contribution Limits: For 2024, the contribution limit is $19,500, with an additional catch-up contribution of $6,500 for those aged 50 and over.

Employer Matching: Many employers offer matching contributions, which are essentially free money for employees.

IRA (Individual Retirement Account):

Traditional IRA: Contributions are tax-deductible, and withdrawals are taxed in retirement.

Roth IRA: Contributions are made with after-tax dollars, and withdrawals are tax-free in retirement.

Contribution Limits: For 2024, the limit is $6,500, with a catch-up contribution of $1,000 for those aged 50 and over.

2. Canada

Registered Retirement Savings Plan (RRSP):

Overview: Tax-advantaged account allowing Canadians to save for retirement.

Tax Benefits: Contributions are tax-deductible, and investments grow tax-deferred until withdrawal.

Contribution Limits: For 2024, the limit is 18% of the previous year's earned income, up to a maximum of CAD 27,830.

Spousal RRSPs: Allow higher-earning spouses to contribute to their partner's RRSP, providing potential tax benefits.

Tax-Free Savings Account (TFSA):

Overview: Allows Canadians to save and invest money tax-free.

Tax Benefits: Contributions are not tax-deductible, but all withdrawals, including investment gains, are tax-free.

Contribution Limits: The annual limit for 2024 is CAD 6,000, with unused contribution room carried forward indefinitely.

3. United Kingdom

Personal Pension Schemes:

Overview: Includes workplace pensions and private pension plans.

Tax Benefits: Contributions are made from pre-tax income, and the government adds tax relief. Investment growth is tax-free, but withdrawals are taxed.

Contribution Limits: Annual allowance of £40,000, with a lifetime allowance of £1,073,100.

Individual Savings Accounts (ISAs):

Overview: Include Cash ISAs and Stocks & Shares ISAs, offering tax-free growth.

Tax Benefits: No tax on income or capital gains within the ISA.

Contribution Limits: The annual limit for 2024 is £20,000.

4. Australia

Superannuation (Super):

Overview: A compulsory retirement savings system where employers contribute a percentage of an employee's earnings to a superannuation fund.

Tax Benefits: Contributions and investment earnings within the super fund are taxed at a reduced rate.

Contribution Limits: Concessional (pre-tax) contributions limit is AUD 27,500 per year. Non-concessional (after-tax) contributions limit is AUD 110,000 per year.

Self-Managed Superannuation Funds (SMSFs):

Overview: Allows individuals to manage their own superannuation investments.

Flexibility: Greater control over investment choices, but requires compliance with regulatory requirements.

Tax Benefits: Same as standard superannuation funds, with tax concessions on contributions and earnings.

5. Germany

Riester Pension:

Overview: Government-subsidized private pension plan designed to supplement the state pension.

Tax Benefits: Contributions are tax-deductible, and the government provides direct subsidies.

Contribution Limits: The maximum subsidized amount is EUR 2,100 per year, including the basic and child allowances.

Rürup Pension (Basisrente):

Overview: A private pension plan for self-employed individuals and high earners.

Tax Benefits: Contributions are tax-deductible, with a portion of the pension taxed upon withdrawal.

Contribution Limits: The maximum deductible contribution is EUR 25,787 for individuals and EUR 51,574 for married couples in 2024.

6. Japan

National Pension System (NPS):

Overview: Mandatory for all residents, providing a basic pension.

Contribution Requirements: Flat-rate contributions for all participants.

Tax Benefits: Contributions are tax-deductible, and benefits are taxable upon receipt.

iDeCo (Individual-type Defined Contribution Pension Plan):

Overview: Voluntary, tax-advantaged pension plan allowing additional savings.

Tax Benefits: Contributions are tax-deductible, and investment gains grow tax-free. Withdrawals are taxed as income.

Contribution Limits: Varies by employment status, with a maximum of JPY 27,600 per month for employees with corporate pensions.

7. India

Employees' Provident Fund (EPF):

Overview: A mandatory retirement savings scheme for salaried employees in the organized sector.

Contribution: Both employer and employee contribute 12% of the employee's basic salary and dearness allowance.

Tax Benefits: Contributions are tax-deductible under Section 80C of the Income Tax Act. Interest earned and withdrawals are tax-free if the employee has completed five years of continuous service.

Interest Rate: The interest rate is set annually by the government and is typically higher than regular savings accounts.

Public Provident Fund (PPF):

Overview: A long-term savings scheme backed by the government, available to all Indian residents.

Contribution Limits: Minimum annual contribution of INR 500 and a maximum of INR 1.5 lakh.

Tax Benefits: Contributions are tax-deductible under Section 80C. Interest earned and maturity proceeds are tax-free.

Tenure: 15 years, with the option to extend in blocks of 5 years.

Interest Rate: The interest rate is reviewed and set by the government every quarter.

National Pension System (NPS):

Overview: A voluntary, defined contribution retirement savings scheme aimed at enabling subscribers to make systematic savings during their working life.

Contribution: No fixed annual contribution limits, but to avail tax benefits, contributions should not exceed 10% of the salary (for employees) or 20% of gross income (for self-employed).

Tax Benefits: Contributions are tax-deductible under Section 80C and an additional deduction of INR 50,000 under Section 80CCD(1B). The maturity corpus is partially tax-free, with 60% of the corpus being tax-free and 40% mandatorily used to purchase an annuity.

Investment Options: Various investment choices including equity, corporate bonds, and government securities managed by professional fund managers.

Flexibility: Subscribers can switch between different fund managers and asset classes.

Atal Pension Yojana (APY):

Overview: A government-backed pension scheme targeted at unorganized sector workers.

Contribution: Fixed monthly contributions depending on the chosen pension amount (ranging from INR 1,000 to INR 5,000 per month) starting from age 18 up to 40.

Tax Benefits: Contributions are eligible for tax benefits under Section 80CCD.

Pension Benefits: Guaranteed minimum monthly pension starting from age 60, based on the contributions made.

Senior Citizens Savings Scheme (SCSS):

Overview: A government-backed savings scheme specifically for senior citizens.

Eligibility: Individuals aged 60 and above, or 55 and above under certain conditions.

Contribution Limits: Maximum investment limit of INR 15 lakh.

Tax Benefits: Contributions are eligible for tax deduction under Section 80C, but interest earned is taxable.

Interest Rate: Typically higher than regular savings accounts, and reviewed quarterly by the government.

Tenure: 5 years, with an option to extend for an additional 3 years.

Conclusion

Retirement accounts differ widely across countries, each offering unique benefits and tax advantages. Understanding these differences can help you optimize your retirement savings strategy. Whether it's taking advantage of employer-sponsored plans, tax-deferred growth, or government subsidies, early and consistent contributions to these accounts are key to building a secure financial future. By leveraging the specific benefits and features of retirement accounts in your country, you can ensure a comfortable and financially stable retirement.

Chapter 8: Long-Term Financial Planning

3. Legacy Planning

Basics of Estate Planning and Ensuring Your Financial Legacy

Legacy planning, or estate planning, is a crucial aspect of long-term financial planning. It involves preparing for the transfer of your assets and wealth to your heirs and beneficiaries after your death.

Effective legacy planning ensures that your financial legacy is preserved, distributed according to your wishes, and can significantly reduce the burden on your loved ones. Here's an in-depth look at the basics of estate planning and how to ensure your financial legacy.

1. Understanding Estate Planning

Definition: Estate planning is the process of arranging the management and disposal of a person's estate during their life and after death.

Goals: The main objectives are to ensure that your assets are distributed according to your wishes, minimize taxes, and provide for your family's financial security.

2. Key Components of Estate Planning

Wills:

Overview: A legal document that specifies how your assets should be distributed after your death.

Importance: Ensures your assets are distributed according to your wishes, names guardians for minor children, and appoints an executor to manage your estate.

Updating: Regularly update your will to reflect changes in your life circumstances, such as marriage, divorce, births, and deaths.

Trusts:

Overview: Legal arrangements where one party holds assets on behalf of another.

Types:

Revocable Trusts: Can be altered or revoked by the grantor during their lifetime.

Irrevocable Trusts: Cannot be changed once established, offering tax benefits and asset protection.

Benefits: Avoid probate, provide privacy, reduce estate taxes, and manage assets for beneficiaries.

Power of Attorney (POA):

Overview: A legal document that gives someone you trust the authority to make decisions on your behalf if you become incapacitated.

Types:

General POA: Grants broad powers over your affairs.

Limited POA: Grants specific powers for a defined task or period.

Durable POA: Remains in effect if you become incapacitated.

Healthcare POA: Authorizes someone to make medical decisions for you if you are unable to do so.

Advance Healthcare Directive (Living Will):

Overview: A legal document outlining your wishes regarding medical treatment if you are unable to communicate them.

Purpose: Ensures your healthcare preferences are known and followed, reducing the burden on family members.

Beneficiary Designations:

Overview: Specifies who will receive assets from accounts such as life insurance policies, retirement accounts, and bank accounts.

Importance: Ensures assets are transferred directly to beneficiaries, bypassing probate.

Letter of Intent:

Overview: A non-legal document that provides additional information and instructions to your executor and beneficiaries.

Contents: Can include funeral arrangements, personal messages, and details about asset distribution.

3. Minimizing Taxes

Estate Taxes: Taxes levied on the transfer of the estate upon death.

Strategies: Establishing trusts, gifting assets during your lifetime, and setting up charitable donations to reduce the taxable estate.

Gift Taxes: Taxes on transfers of money or property to others while you are alive.

Annual Exclusion: In the US, you can give up to a certain amount (e.g., $15,000 per recipient in 2024) without incurring gift taxes.

Generation-Skipping Transfer Tax (GSTT): Additional tax on transfers to grandchildren or unrelated individuals more than 37.5 years younger than you.

Strategies: Using generation-skipping trusts to transfer wealth efficiently.

4. Ensuring Your Financial Legacy

Document Organization: Keep all estate planning documents organized and accessible. Ensure your executor and trusted family members know where to find them.

Professional Guidance: Consult with estate planning attorneys, financial advisors, and tax professionals to create a comprehensive plan tailored to your needs.

Family Communication: Discuss your estate plan with your family to ensure they understand your wishes and reduce potential conflicts.

Regular Review and Updates: Life changes can impact your estate plan. Regularly review and update your plan to reflect new circumstances, such as changes in family structure, financial status, or tax laws.

5. Special Considerations

Business Succession Planning: If you own a business, create a succession plan to ensure a smooth transition and continuity.

Options: Selling the business, transferring ownership to family members, or establishing a management trust.

Charitable Giving: Incorporate charitable donations into your estate plan to support causes important to you and potentially reduce estate taxes.

Vehicles: Charitable trusts, donor-advised funds, and direct bequests.

Conclusion

Legacy planning is a vital part of long-term financial planning, ensuring your assets are distributed according to your wishes and providing financial security for your loved ones. By understanding the key components of estate planning, minimizing taxes, and ensuring thorough documentation and communication, you can establish a comprehensive plan that preserves your financial legacy. Regularly reviewing and updating your estate plan, along with seeking professional guidance, will help adapt to life changes and evolving financial landscapes, ensuring your legacy endures as intended.

Chapter 9: Financial Strategies for Specific Groups

1. Young Adults

Handling Student Loans, Entry-Level Salaries, and First-Time Investing

Navigating financial independence as a young adult can be challenging. This chapter provides practical strategies for managing student loans, making the most of entry-level salaries, and starting your investment journey. Here's a detailed guide to help young adults establish a strong financial foundation.

1. Handling Student Loans

Understanding Your Loans:

Types of Loans: Identify the types of student loans you have (federal vs. private) and their respective terms, interest rates, and repayment options.

Grace Period: Be aware of any grace periods before repayment starts and plan accordingly.

Repayment Strategies:

Standard Repayment Plan: Fixed monthly payments over a 10-year period. This plan ensures the fastest repayment but may have higher monthly payments.

Income-Driven Repayment Plans: Payments based on your income and family size. Plans include Income-Based Repayment (IBR), Pay As You Earn (PAYE), and Revised Pay As You Earn (REPAYE).

Extended Repayment Plan: Extends the repayment period up to 25 years, resulting in lower monthly payments but higher overall interest costs.

Graduated Repayment Plan: Payments start low and increase every two years. This can be useful if you expect your income to rise over time.

Refinancing: Consider refinancing your loans to secure a lower interest rate. Note that refinancing federal loans with a private lender will forfeit federal protections and benefits.

Tips for Efficient Repayment:

Make Extra Payments: Whenever possible, make extra payments towards the principal to reduce the loan balance faster.

Set Up Auto-Pay: Many lenders offer a discount on interest rates if you set up automatic payments.

Employer Assistance: Check if your employer offers student loan repayment assistance as part of your benefits package.

2. Managing Entry-Level Salaries

Budgeting Basics:

Create a Budget: Track your income and expenses to create a realistic budget. Allocate funds for essentials, savings, debt repayment, and discretionary spending.

50/30/20 Rule: A simple budgeting rule where 50% of your income goes to necessities, 30% to discretionary spending, and 20% to savings and debt repayment.

Living Within Your Means:

Avoid Lifestyle Inflation: Resist the temptation to increase your spending as your income rises. Focus on maintaining a modest lifestyle and saving the difference.

Cut Unnecessary Expenses: Identify and eliminate non-essential expenses. This could include dining out less frequently, reducing subscription services, or finding cheaper alternatives for entertainment.

Building an Emergency Fund:

Start Small: Aim to save at least $500 to $1,000 initially to cover minor emergencies.

Set a Goal: Ultimately, build an emergency fund that covers 3-6 months of living expenses. This provides a financial safety net in case of job loss or unexpected expenses.

Automate Savings: Set up automatic transfers to your emergency fund to ensure consistent savings.

3. First-Time Investing

Understanding the Basics:

Investment Vehicles: Familiarize yourself with different investment options such as stocks, bonds, mutual funds, and ETFs.

Risk Tolerance: Assess your risk tolerance to determine the right mix of investments. Generally, younger investors can afford to take on more risk due to a longer investment horizon.

Starting Small:

Begin with Retirement Accounts: Utilize employer-sponsored retirement plans like a 401(k) or individual retirement accounts (IRA). These accounts offer tax advantages and long-term growth potential.

Employer Match: Contribute enough to your 401(k) to get the full employer match, which is essentially free money.

Building a Diversified Portfolio:

Low-Cost Index Funds: Invest in low-cost index funds or ETFs that provide broad market exposure and minimize fees.

Dollar-Cost Averaging: Invest a fixed amount of money regularly, regardless of market conditions. This strategy reduces the impact of market volatility.

Robo-Advisors:

Automated Investing: Consider using robo-advisors, which provide automated, low-cost investment management based on your goals and risk tolerance.

Benefits: Robo-advisors offer diversified portfolios, automatic rebalancing, and tax-loss harvesting.

Continuing Education:

Stay Informed: Continuously educate yourself about personal finance and investing. Utilize online resources, books, podcasts, and financial news to stay updated.

Financial Advisors: If needed, consult with a certified financial planner or advisor to develop a personalized investment strategy.

Conclusion

For young adults, managing student loans, optimizing entry-level salaries, and starting to invest are critical steps toward financial independence. By understanding your student loan options and repayment strategies, living within your means, and beginning to invest wisely, you can build a solid financial foundation. Regularly reviewing and adjusting your financial plan as your circumstances change will help you stay on track and achieve your long-term financial goals.

Chapter 9: Financial Strategies for Specific Groups

2. Single Parents

Budgeting on a Single Income, Finding Financial Aid, and Planning for Children's Future

Managing finances as a single parent can be particularly challenging due to the need to support a family on a single income while planning for both short-term needs and long-term goals. This section provides strategies for effective budgeting, finding financial aid, and planning for your children's future.

1. Budgeting on a Single Income

Creating a Realistic Budget:

Track Your Income and Expenses: Begin by listing all sources of income and tracking every expense. Use budgeting apps or spreadsheets to help categorize spending.

Essential Expenses: Prioritize essential expenses such as housing, utilities, groceries, childcare, and transportation.

Discretionary Spending: Limit non-essential expenses. Look for areas where you can cut back, such as dining out, entertainment, and subscriptions.

50/30/20 Rule for Single Parents:

50% Essentials: Allocate half of your income to necessities.

30% Discretionary: Use this portion for non-essential but desired expenses.

20% Savings and Debt Repayment: Dedicate the remaining portion to savings, emergency funds, and debt repayment.

Emergency Fund:

Start Small: Aim to save a small emergency fund initially, such as $500 to $1,000.

Build Over Time: Work towards saving 3-6 months of living expenses. Automate savings to ensure consistency.

Reducing Expenses:

Childcare Costs: Look for affordable childcare options, such as community programs, cooperative childcare, or subsidies.

Housing: Consider downsizing, moving to a more affordable area, or sharing housing costs with a roommate or family member.

Utilities and Groceries: Save on utilities by being energy-efficient and reduce grocery bills by meal planning, buying in bulk, and using coupons.

2. Finding Financial Aid

Government Assistance Programs:

Supplemental Nutrition Assistance Program (SNAP): Provides food assistance for low-income families.

Temporary Assistance for Needy Families (TANF): Offers financial assistance and support services for families in need.

Childcare Subsidies: Many states offer subsidies to help cover the cost of childcare for low-income families.

Medicaid and CHIP: Provide health coverage for low-income parents and children.

Scholarships and Grants:

Educational Grants: Look for federal and state grants for single parents returning to school, such as the Federal Pell Grant.

Scholarships: Search for scholarships specifically aimed at single parents or their children. Websites like Fastweb and Scholarships.com can be useful resources.

Local Resources: Community organizations, local charities, and religious institutions may offer financial assistance, scholarships, or grants.

Nonprofit Organizations:

Single Parent Support Groups: Many nonprofits offer financial support, counseling, and resources for single parents. Organizations such as Single Parent Advocate and Helping Hands for Single Moms can provide valuable assistance.

Food Banks and Clothing Assistance: Local food banks, clothing pantries, and thrift stores can help reduce basic living costs.

3. Planning for Children's Future

Education Savings:

529 College Savings Plans: Tax-advantaged savings plans designed to encourage saving for future education costs. Contributions grow

tax-free, and withdrawals for qualified education expenses are also tax-free.

Coverdell Education Savings Account (ESA): Another tax-advantaged account for education expenses, including primary, secondary, and college expenses.

Roth IRA: Though primarily a retirement account, Roth IRAs can be used for education expenses without penalties under certain conditions.

Life Insurance:

Term Life Insurance: Affordable coverage that provides financial protection for a specified term. Ensures your children are financially secure if something happens to you.

Whole Life Insurance: Provides lifelong coverage and can build cash value over time, but is generally more expensive than term life insurance.

Estate Planning:

Wills and Trusts: Create a will to specify guardianship and distribution of assets. Consider a trust to manage and protect assets for your children.

Beneficiary Designations: Ensure life insurance policies, retirement accounts, and other assets have updated beneficiary designations.

Teaching Financial Literacy:

Basic Money Management: Teach your children the importance of budgeting, saving, and responsible spending.

Age-Appropriate Lessons: Use allowances, savings jars, and simple budgeting tools to instill good financial habits from an early age.

Involving Children in Budgeting: Involve older children in the family budgeting process to help them understand financial constraints and priorities.

Conclusion

Single parents face unique financial challenges, but with careful planning and resourcefulness, it is possible to create a stable and secure financial future. By creating a realistic budget, finding financial aid, and planning for your children's future, single parents can achieve financial independence and provide a solid foundation for their family. Regularly revisiting and adjusting your financial plan as circumstances change will help ensure long-term financial stability and security.

Chapter 9: Financial Strategies for Specific Groups

3. Freelancers and Gig Workers

Managing Irregular Income, Taxes, and Saving for Retirement

Freelancers and gig workers face unique financial challenges due to their irregular income streams and lack of employer-provided benefits. This chapter provides strategies for effectively managing irregular income, staying on top of taxes, and saving for retirement.

1. Managing Irregular Income

Creating a Variable Budget:

Base Your Budget on Minimum Expected Income: Calculate the minimum income you expect to earn each month and create a budget based on this amount. This ensures you can cover essential expenses even during low-earning periods.

Separate Fixed and Variable Expenses: Identify your fixed expenses (e.g., rent, utilities, insurance) and variable expenses (e.g., groceries, entertainment). Prioritize covering fixed expenses first.

Establish a Buffer Fund: Create a buffer fund to cover months when your income falls short. Aim to save at least 3-6 months' worth of expenses in this fund.

Income Smoothing Strategies:

Save Surplus Income: When you have a good month, save the surplus to cover leaner months. Transfer the excess to your buffer fund or a separate savings account.

Consistent Withdrawal Plan: Pay yourself a fixed amount each month from your business account to your personal account. This simulates a regular paycheck and helps manage personal expenses more predictably.

Invoicing and Payment Practices:

Set Clear Payment Terms: Ensure your contracts clearly state payment terms, including due dates, late fees, and preferred payment methods.

Prompt Invoicing: Invoice clients as soon as the work is completed. Consider using invoicing software to streamline the process.

Follow Up on Late Payments: Establish a follow-up system for overdue invoices. Regularly remind clients about outstanding payments.

2. Taxes

Understanding Tax Obligations:

Self-Employment Tax: Freelancers and gig workers must pay self-employment tax, which covers Social Security and Medicare. This is in addition to regular income tax.

Quarterly Estimated Taxes: To avoid penalties, estimate and pay taxes quarterly. Use IRS Form 1040-ES to calculate and submit these payments.

Record Keeping:

Track Income and Expenses: Maintain detailed records of all income and business-related expenses. Use accounting software or apps to simplify tracking.

Keep Receipts and Invoices: Store digital copies of receipts, invoices, and other relevant documents for at least seven years.

Separate Business and Personal Finances: Use a separate bank account for business transactions to simplify tracking and reporting.

Tax Deductions:

Home Office Deduction: If you use a portion of your home exclusively for business, you may qualify for a home office deduction. Calculate this based on the square footage of your office relative to your home.

Business Expenses: Deduct ordinary and necessary business expenses such as office supplies, software, marketing costs, and professional services.

Health Insurance Premiums: Deduct premiums paid for health insurance for yourself and your family.

Hiring a Tax Professional:

Expert Guidance: Consider hiring a CPA or tax advisor familiar with freelance and gig work. They can help you maximize deductions and ensure compliance with tax laws.

Tax Planning: Work with a tax professional to develop a tax strategy that minimizes your liability and helps you plan for future tax obligations.

3. Saving for Retirement

Retirement Accounts for Freelancers:

SEP-IRA (Simplified Employee Pension Individual Retirement Account): Allows you to contribute up to 25% of your net earnings from self-employment, up to a maximum limit ($66,000 for 2023).

Solo 401(k): Offers higher contribution limits, combining employee and employer contributions. You can contribute up to $22,500 as an employee (or $30,000 if over 50), plus up to 25% of your net self-employment income as an employer.

Traditional or Roth IRA: Contribute up to $6,500 per year ($7,500 if over 50). Traditional IRAs offer tax-deductible contributions, while Roth IRAs offer tax-free withdrawals in retirement.

Automating Savings:

Regular Contributions: Set up automatic transfers from your business account to your retirement accounts. Treat these contributions as a non-negotiable expense.

Increase Contributions Gradually: As your income grows, increase your retirement contributions. Aim to maximize annual contribution limits when possible.

Investment Strategies:

Diversified Portfolio: Spread your investments across different asset classes (stocks, bonds, real estate) to reduce risk.

Low-Cost Index Funds: Consider investing in low-cost index funds or ETFs to minimize fees and ensure broad market exposure.

Rebalance Periodically: Regularly review and adjust your portfolio to maintain your desired asset allocation.

4. Health and Disability Insurance

Health Insurance:

Marketplace Plans: Purchase health insurance through the Health Insurance Marketplace if you don't have access to employer-provided plans.

Subsidies and Tax Credits: Check if you qualify for subsidies or tax credits to reduce premium costs based on your income level.

Disability Insurance:

Importance of Coverage: Protect your income in case of illness or injury that prevents you from working. Consider short-term and long-term disability policies.

Policy Options: Compare policies to find one that fits your needs and budget. Look for policies with own-occupation coverage, which pays benefits if you cannot perform your specific job.

Conclusion

Freelancers and gig workers must take proactive steps to manage irregular income, stay on top of taxes, and save for retirement. By creating a variable budget, maintaining thorough records, leveraging tax deductions, and investing in appropriate retirement accounts, they can build a stable financial future. Additionally, securing health and disability insurance will protect against unforeseen circumstances, ensuring long-term financial security. Regularly reviewing and adjusting financial strategies will help freelancers and gig workers stay on track and adapt to changing circumstances.

Chapter 9: Financial Strategies for Specific Groups

4. Retirees or Near-Retirees

Maximizing Retirement Income, Managing Healthcare Costs, and Legacy Planning

As individuals approach or enter retirement, financial strategies need to focus on maximizing income, managing healthcare expenses, and planning for their legacy. This chapter provides practical advice to help retirees and near-retirees navigate these critical areas to ensure financial security and peace of mind.

1. Maximizing Retirement Income

Social Security Optimization:

Timing Your Benefits: Understand the impact of claiming Social Security at different ages. Delaying benefits beyond full retirement age can increase your monthly payments significantly.

Spousal Benefits: Explore spousal benefits if you are married. You may be eligible for a higher benefit based on your spouse's earnings record.

Working in Retirement: Be aware of how working while receiving benefits can affect your Social Security payments. There are earnings limits before full retirement age that could reduce your benefits temporarily.

Pension Plans:

Understanding Payout Options: If you have a pension, carefully consider the payout options, such as lump-sum versus annuity payments. An annuity can provide a steady income stream for life.

Cost-of-Living Adjustments (COLA): Check if your pension includes COLA, which helps your income keep pace with inflation.

Investment Withdrawals:

Safe Withdrawal Rate: Follow the 4% rule as a starting point, which suggests withdrawing 4% of your retirement portfolio annually to reduce the risk of depleting your savings.

Bucket Strategy: Use a bucket strategy to manage investments and withdrawals. Divide your portfolio into short-term (cash and bonds), medium-term (bonds and balanced funds), and long-term (stocks and growth funds) buckets to manage risk and liquidity.

Annuities:

Immediate Annuities: Consider purchasing an immediate annuity to convert a lump sum into a guaranteed income stream.

Deferred Annuities: Explore deferred annuities to start receiving payments at a later date, which can provide additional income in later years.

2. Managing Healthcare Costs

Medicare:

Enrollment Periods: Enroll in Medicare during the initial enrollment period (three months before turning 65 to three months after your 65th birthday) to avoid late enrollment penalties.

Parts of Medicare: Understand the different parts of Medicare: Part A (hospital insurance), Part B (medical insurance), Part C (Medicare Advantage plans), and Part D (prescription drug coverage).

Supplemental Insurance: Consider a Medigap policy to cover out-of-pocket costs not covered by Medicare. Compare different plans to find one that suits your needs.

Long-Term Care Insurance:

Coverage Options: Evaluate long-term care insurance options to cover the costs of extended care in nursing homes, assisted living facilities, or at home.

When to Buy: Purchase long-term care insurance while you are still in good health and before premium costs become prohibitive.

Health Savings Accounts (HSAs):

Tax Benefits: If you are eligible for an HSA, contribute to it for tax-free savings that can be used to pay for qualified medical expenses.

Using HSA Funds: After age 65, HSA funds can be used for non-medical expenses without penalty, though they will be subject to income tax.

Managing Out-of-Pocket Costs:

Preventive Care: Take advantage of preventive care services covered by Medicare to maintain your health and catch potential issues early.

Generic Medications: Opt for generic medications when possible to save on prescription costs.

Shop Around: Compare prices for medical procedures and prescriptions at different providers and pharmacies to find the best deals.

3. Legacy Planning

Estate Planning:

Wills and Trusts: Create or update your will to ensure your assets are distributed according to your wishes. Consider setting up trusts to manage and protect assets for your heirs.

Beneficiary Designations: Regularly review and update beneficiary designations on retirement accounts, life insurance policies, and other financial accounts.

Power of Attorney and Healthcare Directives: Appoint a durable power of attorney for financial matters and a healthcare proxy to make medical decisions on your behalf if you are unable to do so.

Minimizing Estate Taxes:

Gifting Strategies: Use annual gifting exclusions to transfer wealth to heirs without incurring gift taxes. As of 2024, you can give up to $17,000 per recipient per year without tax consequences.

Charitable Contributions: Make charitable donations to reduce the size of your taxable estate and benefit causes you care about.

Legacy Planning Tools:

Life Insurance: Use life insurance to provide financial support for your dependents and cover estate taxes or debts.

Qualified Longevity Annuity Contracts (QLACs): Invest in a QLAC to provide a guaranteed income stream later in life, reducing the amount required to withdraw from other retirement accounts.

Communication with Heirs:

Discuss Plans Openly: Communicate your estate plans with your heirs to ensure they understand your wishes and the reasons behind them.

Financial Education: Educate your heirs about managing inherited wealth responsibly to help them preserve and grow their inheritance.

Conclusion

Retirees and near-retirees need to adopt strategies that maximize retirement income, manage healthcare costs effectively, and plan their legacy thoughtfully. By optimizing Social Security benefits, managing investments wisely, understanding healthcare options, and creating a comprehensive estate plan, retirees can ensure financial stability and peace of mind. Regularly reviewing and adjusting these strategies will help adapt to changes in financial circumstances and personal goals, providing a secure and fulfilling retirement.

Chapter 9: Financial Strategies for Specific Groups

5. Minorities and Underrepresented Groups

Overcoming Financial Barriers, Accessing Resources, and Building Community Wealth

Minorities and underrepresented groups often face unique financial challenges due to systemic barriers, limited access to resources, and historical inequalities. This chapter provides strategies to overcome these barriers, access available resources, and build wealth within these communities.

1. Overcoming Financial Barriers

Addressing Discrimination in Financial Services:

Know Your Rights: Understand your rights under laws such as the Equal Credit Opportunity Act (ECOA) and the Fair Housing Act, which prohibit discrimination in lending and housing.

Advocacy and Support: Seek support from organizations like the NAACP, Urban League, and other advocacy groups that fight for financial equality and provide resources and education.

Building and Improving Credit:

Credit Education: Learn about credit scores, how they are calculated, and their importance. Use resources from organizations like Credit Builders Alliance and local community development financial institutions (CDFIs).

Secured Credit Cards: Use secured credit cards to build or rebuild credit. Make small purchases and pay off the balance in full each month to establish a positive payment history.

Credit Counseling Services: Work with reputable credit counseling agencies to develop a plan for improving your credit score and managing debt.

Navigating Predatory Lending:

Identify Predatory Practices: Recognize red flags of predatory lending, such as high fees, excessive interest rates, and pressure to take on unaffordable loans.

Alternative Financial Services: Use community-based financial institutions, credit unions, and CDFIs that offer fair and transparent lending products.

2. Accessing Resources

Financial Education Programs:

Community Workshops: Participate in financial literacy workshops offered by community organizations, nonprofits, and local government agencies.

Online Resources: Utilize free online resources, courses, and webinars from reputable sources like Khan Academy, Consumer Financial Protection Bureau (CFPB), and MyMoney.gov.

Grants and Scholarships:

Educational Grants: Explore grants and scholarships specifically aimed at minorities and underrepresented groups to support higher education and vocational training.

Business Grants: Apply for grants designed to support minority-owned businesses, such as those offered by the Minority Business Development Agency (MBDA) and private foundations.

Government Programs and Assistance:

Small Business Administration (SBA): Access SBA programs that provide loans, mentorship, and training for minority entrepreneurs.

Housing Assistance: Utilize federal and state programs like the Housing Choice Voucher Program (Section 8) and down payment assistance programs aimed at first-time homebuyers.

3. Building Community Wealth

Investing in Local Businesses:

Support Minority-Owned Businesses: Make a conscious effort to buy from and invest in minority-owned businesses. This helps circulate money within the community and fosters economic growth.

Cooperative Businesses: Consider forming or investing in cooperative businesses, which are owned and operated by members of the community, ensuring profits stay local.

Community Development Financial Institutions (CDFIs):

Access to Capital: Utilize CDFIs, which provide financial products and services to underserved communities. They offer fair loans, financial education, and business development support.

Local Investment: Support CDFIs through deposits or investments to help them grow and expand their services within the community.

Real Estate and Homeownership:

Homeownership Programs: Participate in homeownership programs that provide education, counseling, and financial assistance to first-time homebuyers.

Community Land Trusts (CLTs): Explore CLTs, which provide affordable housing by owning the land and selling the home to individuals. This model helps maintain long-term affordability and community stability.

Education and Mentorship:

Financial Literacy Programs: Implement financial literacy programs in schools and community centers to educate the next generation on money management, investing, and entrepreneurship.

Mentorship Networks: Develop mentorship networks that connect experienced professionals with young people and aspiring entrepreneurs within the community.

Policy Advocacy:

Community Organizing: Engage in community organizing to advocate for policies that address economic disparities and promote financial inclusion.

Coalitions and Alliances: Join coalitions and alliances that work towards economic justice and equity at local, state, and national levels.

Conclusion

Minorities and underrepresented groups can overcome financial barriers by leveraging available resources, improving financial literacy, and advocating for equitable policies. By focusing on building credit, accessing grants and scholarships, utilizing CDFIs, and supporting local businesses, these groups can create sustainable wealth and economic growth within their communities. Through collective effort and strategic planning, it is possible to achieve financial independence and stability, fostering a more inclusive and equitable economic landscape. Regularly revisiting and updating financial strategies will help adapt to changing circumstances and continue building community wealth over time.

Chapter 10: Tools and Resources

1. Financial Tools

Recommended Apps and Software for Budgeting, Investing, and Tracking Finances

Leveraging the right financial tools can significantly enhance your ability to manage money, invest wisely, and track financial progress. This section provides an overview of recommended apps and software for budgeting, investing, and financial tracking, making it easier to stay organized and make informed financial decisions.

Budgeting Tools

Mint:

Overview: Mint is a free budgeting app that aggregates all your financial accounts, tracks your spending, and helps you create budgets.

Features: Automatic categorization of transactions, bill reminders, and customizable budget goals.

Benefits: User-friendly interface, comprehensive financial overview, and personalized tips for saving money.

YNAB (You Need A Budget):

Overview: YNAB is a paid app designed to help you allocate every dollar you earn, encouraging proactive budgeting and financial planning.

Features: Real-time expense tracking, goal-setting, and detailed reports on spending patterns.

Benefits: Strong focus on financial education, helpful budgeting workshops, and a supportive community.

PocketGuard:

Overview: PocketGuard simplifies budgeting by showing you how much disposable income you have after accounting for bills and savings goals.

Features: Automated tracking, spending insights, and customizable categories.

Benefits: Easy-to-understand dashboard, helps avoid overspending, and encourages saving.

Investing Tools

Robinhood:

Overview: Robinhood is a popular app that offers commission-free trading for stocks, ETFs, options, and cryptocurrencies.

Features: Real-time market data, customizable watchlists, and educational resources for new investors.

Benefits: User-friendly interface, no trading fees, and fractional shares availability.

Betterment:

Overview: Betterment is a robo-advisor that provides automated investing services, tailored portfolios, and personalized financial advice.

Features: Goal-based investing, tax-efficient strategies, and retirement planning tools.

Benefits: Low management fees, automatic portfolio rebalancing, and financial planning support.

Acorns:

Overview: Acorns rounds up your everyday purchases to the nearest dollar and invests the spare change into diversified portfolios.

Features: Round-ups, recurring investments, and retirement account options.

Benefits: Easy way to start investing with small amounts, educational content, and automated savings.

Tracking Finances

Personal Capital:

Overview: Personal Capital offers free financial tools for tracking net worth, investments, and retirement planning, along with a paid advisory service.

Features: Comprehensive dashboard, investment performance analysis, and retirement planner.

Benefits: Detailed financial insights, personalized advice, and robust security measures.

Quicken:

Overview: Quicken is a long-standing financial management software that provides tools for budgeting, tracking investments, and managing personal finances.

Features: Bill management, investment tracking, debt reduction planner, and tax reporting.

Benefits: Comprehensive features, historical data tracking, and compatibility with various financial institutions.

Tiller Money:

Overview: Tiller Money uses spreadsheets to track your finances, combining the flexibility of Excel and Google Sheets with automated financial data updates.

Features: Automated transaction import, customizable templates, and daily email summaries.

Benefits: Highly customizable, detailed financial tracking, and integrates with Google Sheets and Excel.

Conclusion

Selecting the right financial tools is essential for effective money management. Whether you're looking to create a budget, invest wisely, or track your financial progress, the recommended apps and software provide a range of features to meet your needs. Mint, YNAB, and PocketGuard are excellent for budgeting; Robinhood, Betterment, and Acorns facilitate investing; and Personal Capital, Quicken, and Tiller Money offer comprehensive financial tracking solutions. By utilizing these tools, you can gain greater control over your finances, make informed decisions, and work towards achieving financial independence and security.

Chapter 10: Tools and Resources

2. Books and Websites

Further Reading and Reliable Online Resources for Financial Education

Continuing your financial education is key to achieving and maintaining financial independence. This section highlights essential books and websites that provide valuable insights and practical advice on personal finance, investing, and wealth building. These resources are highly regarded and cover a wide range of financial topics to suit various learning needs and preferences.

Books

"Rich Dad Poor Dad" by Robert Kiyosaki:

Overview: This classic book contrasts the financial philosophies of Kiyosaki's "rich dad" and "poor dad" and emphasizes the importance of financial education and investing.

Key Takeaways: Understanding assets and liabilities, the value of financial independence, and the mindset of wealth-building.

"The Total Money Makeover" by Dave Ramsey:

Overview: Dave Ramsey's step-by-step guide to financial health covers budgeting, debt elimination, and building wealth.

Key Takeaways: The "Baby Steps" program, importance of emergency funds, and debt snowball method.

"Your Money or Your Life" by Vicki Robin and Joe Dominguez:

Overview: This book provides a holistic approach to personal finance, focusing on transforming your relationship with money and achieving financial independence.

Key Takeaways: Tracking expenses, calculating real hourly wage, and achieving financial independence through mindful spending.

"The Intelligent Investor" by Benjamin Graham:

Overview: A seminal book on value investing, offering strategies for achieving long-term investment success.

Key Takeaways: Principles of value investing, margin of safety, and the difference between investing and speculating.

"I Will Teach You to Be Rich" by Ramit Sethi:

Overview: A practical guide for millennials on managing personal finances, including earning more, saving, and investing.

Key Takeaways: Automation of finances, conscious spending, and smart investment strategies.

"The Simple Path to Wealth" by JL Collins:

Overview: This book simplifies the path to financial independence through sensible investing and frugal living.

Key Takeaways: Importance of index funds, benefits of financial independence, and straightforward investing advice.

Websites

Investopedia:

Overview: A comprehensive financial education website offering articles, tutorials, and dictionary entries on a wide range of financial topics.

Key Features: Investment guides, financial calculators, and up-to-date market news.

NerdWallet:

Overview: A personal finance website providing advice on banking, credit cards, loans, investing, and more.

Key Features: Comparisons of financial products, budgeting tips, and investment advice.

The Balance:

Overview: Offers practical advice on personal finance, including budgeting, saving, investing, and retirement planning.

Key Features: Step-by-step guides, expert tips, and informative articles.

Bogleheads:

Overview: A community-driven site inspired by the investment philosophy of John C. Bogle, founder of Vanguard.

Key Features: Forums, investment strategies, and personal finance advice focused on low-cost investing.

Mr. Money Mustache:

Overview: A blog that promotes financial independence through frugality, self-sufficiency, and smart investing.

Key Features: Personal finance articles, practical saving tips, and success stories.

Financial Samurai:

Overview: Provides insights on personal finance, investing, career strategies, and real estate.

Key Features: In-depth articles, case studies, and financial product reviews.

Conclusion

Books and websites are invaluable resources for anyone looking to expand their financial knowledge and skills. By reading renowned books like "Rich Dad Poor Dad" and "The Intelligent Investor," and utilizing trusted websites such as Investopedia and NerdWallet, you can gain a deeper understanding of personal finance, investing, and wealth-building strategies. Continuously educating yourself with these resources will empower you to make informed financial decisions and work towards achieving long-term financial independence and security.

Chapter 10: Tools and Resources

3. Community Support

Importance of Building a Support Network and Finding Financial Mentors

Building a strong support network and finding financial mentors are critical components of achieving financial independence. Community support can provide guidance, encouragement, and accountability, while mentors offer personalized advice and share their experiences. This section elaborates on the importance of these elements and how to effectively seek out and leverage them.

Importance of Building a Support Network

Shared Knowledge and Resources:

Information Exchange: A support network allows for the exchange of financial knowledge and resources, such as tips on budgeting, saving, and investing.

Collective Learning: Group discussions and workshops can facilitate collective learning, where individuals share their experiences and learn from one another's successes and mistakes.

Encouragement and Accountability:

Motivation: Being part of a community of like-minded individuals can provide motivation and encouragement, helping you stay committed to your financial goals.

Accountability Partners: Accountability partners can help you stay on track by regularly checking in on your progress, offering support, and holding you accountable for your financial decisions.

Emotional Support:

Reducing Stress: Financial challenges can be stressful and isolating. Having a support network can provide emotional comfort and reduce feelings of isolation.

Building Confidence: Sharing successes and challenges within a supportive community can boost your confidence and reinforce positive financial behaviors.

Networking Opportunities:

Professional Connections: A strong support network can offer valuable professional connections, opening doors to new job opportunities, partnerships, and financial advice.

Resource Sharing: Members of your network may share resources such as financial advisors, educational tools, and investment opportunities.

Finding Financial Mentors

Why Mentors Matter:

Experience and Insight: Financial mentors have valuable experience and insights that can help you navigate complex financial decisions and avoid common pitfalls.

Personalized Guidance: Mentors can provide tailored advice based on your specific financial situation, goals, and challenges.

Long-Term Growth: A mentor can guide you through different stages of your financial journey, helping you adapt your strategies as your circumstances evolve.

How to Find a Financial Mentor:

Professional Organizations: Join professional organizations and associations related to finance and your industry. These organizations often have mentorship programs and networking events.

Local Community Groups: Participate in local community groups and financial literacy workshops, where you can meet experienced individuals willing to offer guidance.

Online Communities: Engage with online forums, social media groups, and virtual mentorship platforms dedicated to personal finance and investing.

Financial Advisors: Seek out reputable financial advisors who offer mentorship as part of their services. Look for advisors with a fiduciary responsibility to act in your best interest.

Building a Mentorship Relationship:

Be Clear About Your Goals: Clearly communicate your financial goals and what you hope to achieve through the mentorship.

Show Commitment: Demonstrate your commitment to learning and implementing the advice given by your mentor.

Maintain Regular Contact: Schedule regular meetings or check-ins with your mentor to discuss your progress and seek guidance.

Be Open to Feedback: Be receptive to constructive feedback and willing to make necessary changes to your financial habits and strategies.

Leveraging Community and Mentor Support

Engage Actively:

Participate in Events: Attend community events, workshops, and webinars to stay engaged and continually learn.

Contribute to Discussions: Actively contribute to discussions within your network, sharing your experiences and insights while learning from others.

Seek Regular Advice: Regularly seek advice and feedback from your mentor and other trusted members of your support network.

Set Realistic Expectations:

Small Steps: Understand that financial independence is a gradual process. Set realistic short-term goals that contribute to your long-term objectives.

Celebrate Milestones: Celebrate small victories and milestones along the way to stay motivated and positive.

Adapt and Evolve:

Stay Flexible: Be open to adjusting your strategies based on new insights and changing circumstances.

Continuous Learning: Commit to continuous learning and self-improvement through your community and mentor relationships.

Conclusion

Building a support network and finding financial mentors are essential steps towards achieving financial independence. Community support offers shared knowledge, encouragement, and accountability, while mentors provide personalized guidance and insight. By actively engaging with these resources, setting realistic goals, and staying committed to continuous learning, you can navigate the complexities of personal finance with confidence and support. This collaborative approach not only enhances your financial literacy and skills but also empowers you to make informed decisions and achieve long-term financial stability.

Chapter 11: Real-Life Success Stories

1. Case Studies

Inspirational Stories from Individuals in Each Target Group Who Achieved Financial Independence

Learning from those who have successfully navigated their path to financial independence can provide valuable insights and motivation. This section presents inspirational case studies from individuals in various target groups, highlighting their strategies, challenges, and achievements. Each story demonstrates that financial independence is attainable, regardless of one's starting point.

Young Adults

Case Study: Sarah's Journey to Financial Independence

Background: Sarah graduated from college with $30,000 in student loans and a modest entry-level salary.

Challenges: Managing student loan debt, high living expenses in a metropolitan area, and limited financial knowledge.

Strategies:

Budgeting and Saving: Sarah used a budgeting app (YNAB) to track her expenses and save aggressively. She cut unnecessary expenses and focused on needs over wants.

Income Enhancement: To supplement her income, Sarah took on freelance graphic design projects and started a blog about personal finance.

Debt Repayment: She applied the debt avalanche method, prioritizing high-interest loans first while making minimum payments on the rest.

Investing Early: Sarah started investing small amounts in a Roth IRA and took advantage of her employer's 401(k) match.

Outcome: Within five years, Sarah paid off her student loans, built an emergency fund, and accumulated significant savings for retirement. She now shares her journey through her blog, inspiring other young adults to take control of their finances.

Single Parents

Case Study: Maria's Path to Financial Stability

Background: Maria, a single mother of two, struggled with managing household expenses on a single income.

Challenges: High childcare costs, limited income, and lack of financial support.

Strategies:

Budget Optimization: Maria created a strict budget, prioritizing essential expenses and finding ways to reduce costs, such as using coupons and shopping sales.

Financial Aid: She researched and applied for financial assistance programs, including food stamps and childcare subsidies.

Side Hustles: Maria started a home-based business making and selling crafts online, which provided additional income and flexibility.

Education and Career Advancement: She pursued online courses to improve her skills and secure a higher-paying job in her field.

Outcome: Maria achieved financial stability, built a savings cushion, and began contributing to a college fund for her children. Her story is a testament to resilience and resourcefulness, showing other single parents that financial independence is possible with determination and strategic planning.

Freelancers and Gig Workers

Case Study: John's Freelance Success

Background: John transitioned from a corporate job to full-time freelancing in web development.

Challenges: Irregular income, managing taxes, and securing health insurance.

Strategies:

Income Diversification: John diversified his income streams by working on multiple freelance platforms, offering web development, consulting, and online courses.

Financial Management: He used financial tools like QuickBooks to track income and expenses, and set aside a portion of his earnings for taxes.

Savings and Investments: John prioritized building an emergency fund to buffer against income fluctuations and invested in a SEP IRA for retirement savings.

Professional Networking: He joined professional associations and attended industry conferences to expand his network and secure higher-paying contracts.

Outcome: John achieved a stable and thriving freelance career, with a steady stream of clients and a well-managed financial plan. His story encourages other freelancers to manage their finances proactively and seek opportunities for growth.

Retirees or Near-Retirees

Case Study: Linda's Retirement Reimagined

Background: Linda, approaching retirement age, realized she had not saved enough to maintain her desired lifestyle.

Challenges: Insufficient retirement savings, concerns about healthcare costs, and uncertainty about Social Security benefits.

Strategies:

Downsizing: Linda downsized her home to reduce living expenses and free up equity for savings.

Part-Time Work: She took on a part-time job related to her passion for gardening, which provided additional income and kept her active.

Financial Planning: Linda consulted with a financial advisor to optimize her Social Security benefits and create a sustainable withdrawal plan from her retirement accounts.

Healthcare Management: She researched and selected a Medicare plan that balanced cost and coverage, and started a Health Savings Account (HSA).

Outcome: Linda was able to retire comfortably, supplementing her savings with part-time income and enjoying a lower-cost lifestyle. Her experience highlights the importance of adaptability and proactive planning for those nearing retirement.

Minorities and Underrepresented Groups

Case Study: Mark's Community-Centric Wealth Building

Background: Mark, from a minority background, faced systemic financial barriers but was determined to achieve financial independence.

Challenges: Limited access to capital, discriminatory practices in financial services, and lack of representation.

Strategies:

Community Involvement: Mark became active in local financial literacy programs, both as a participant and later as a mentor.

Business Ownership: He started a small business with the support of a Community Development Financial Institution (CDFI) that offered fair lending terms and business development resources.

Financial Education: Mark educated himself on personal finance through books, online courses, and mentorship from successful minority entrepreneurs.

Investing in Real Estate: He invested in affordable real estate within his community, providing both rental income and contributing to community revitalization.

Outcome: Mark built a successful business, acquired multiple rental properties, and created a local scholarship fund for young entrepreneurs. His journey demonstrates the power of community support and the impact of giving back.

Conclusion

These case studies show that financial independence is achievable for individuals from diverse backgrounds and situations. Whether dealing with student debt, managing a single-income household, navigating the uncertainties of freelancing, preparing for retirement, or overcoming systemic barriers, these inspirational stories provide practical strategies and hope. By learning from these examples, readers can find motivation and actionable advice tailored to their unique circumstances, empowering them to take control of their financial future.

Chapter 11: Real-Life Success Stories

2. Lessons Learned

Key Takeaways and Practical Advice from Each Story

Reflecting on the real-life success stories of individuals who achieved financial independence, there are several key lessons and practical pieces of advice that can help guide others on their financial journeys. These insights provide actionable steps that can be applied across different situations and target groups.

Young Adults: Sarah's Journey to Financial Independence

Start Early: Begin budgeting, saving, and investing as soon as possible, even with small amounts.

Practical Advice: Use budgeting apps to track expenses and automate savings to ensure consistent progress.

Diversify Income: Look for side hustles or freelance opportunities to supplement your main income.

Practical Advice: Identify skills that can be monetized and explore platforms like Upwork or Fiverr to find gigs.

Focus on Debt Repayment: Prioritize high-interest debt to reduce overall financial burden.

Practical Advice: Use the debt avalanche method to pay off debts more efficiently, starting with the highest interest rates.

Single Parents: Maria's Path to Financial Stability

Budgeting is Crucial: Create and stick to a strict budget to manage expenses effectively.

Practical Advice: Utilize budgeting tools and apps, and review your budget regularly to make adjustments as needed.

Seek Financial Assistance: Research and apply for available financial aid programs to ease financial pressure.

Practical Advice: Look into government assistance programs, local charities, and scholarships for single parents.

Explore Flexible Income Options: Find side hustles or home-based businesses that offer flexibility.

Practical Advice: Consider online businesses, freelance work, or selling handmade products on platforms like Etsy.

Freelancers and Gig Workers: John's Freelance Success

Diversify Income Streams: Don't rely on a single source of income; spread out your income sources to mitigate risk.

Practical Advice: Offer a variety of services and leverage multiple freelance platforms to attract more clients.

Financial Management Tools: Use financial software to keep track of income, expenses, and taxes.

Practical Advice: Tools like QuickBooks can help manage your finances efficiently and simplify tax preparation.

Save for Uncertain Times: Build an emergency fund to cover periods of irregular income.

Practical Advice: Aim to save at least three to six months' worth of living expenses in an easily accessible account.

Retirees or Near-Retirees: Linda's Retirement Reimagined

Downsize to Save: Consider downsizing your home or living expenses to free up equity and reduce costs.

Practical Advice: Evaluate your housing needs and explore smaller, more affordable living options.

Part-Time Work: Find part-time work that aligns with your interests to supplement retirement income.

Practical Advice: Look for flexible, enjoyable part-time jobs that can provide additional income without significant stress.

Optimize Retirement Benefits: Plan strategically to maximize Social Security and other retirement benefits.

Practical Advice: Consult a financial advisor to understand the best time to start taking Social Security and how to manage your retirement accounts.

Minorities and Underrepresented Groups: Mark's Community-Centric Wealth Building

Community Support: Engage with community organizations that offer financial education and resources.

Practical Advice: Participate in local financial literacy programs and seek mentorship from successful community members.

Access Fair Financing: Utilize Community Development Financial Institutions (CDFIs) for fair lending and business support.

Practical Advice: Research CDFIs in your area that provide small business loans and financial education resources.

Invest in Community: Focus on investments that not only build personal wealth but also support community development.

Practical Advice: Consider real estate investments in local, underserved areas to both generate income and contribute to revitalization efforts.

Universal Lessons Learned

Continuous Education: Keep learning about personal finance through books, courses, and reputable online resources.

Practical Advice: Dedicate time each month to reading financial books or taking online courses to enhance your financial knowledge.

Networking and Mentorship: Build a network of supportive individuals and seek out financial mentors.

Practical Advice: Join professional groups, attend financial seminars, and actively seek mentors who can provide guidance and accountability.

Set Realistic Goals: Establish clear, achievable financial goals and create a plan to reach them.

Practical Advice: Use the SMART criteria (Specific, Measurable, Achievable, Relevant, Time-bound) to set and track your financial goals.

Stay Disciplined and Adaptable: Maintain discipline in your financial habits and be ready to adapt your strategies as needed.

Practical Advice: Regularly review your financial plan and adjust based on changing circumstances or new opportunities.

Conclusion

These real-life success stories and the lessons learned from them illustrate that achieving financial independence is possible for anyone, regardless of their starting point. By applying these practical strategies and maintaining a disciplined, proactive approach to managing finances, individuals can overcome challenges and work towards long-term financial stability and independence.

1. Summary of Key Principles

This book has provided a comprehensive guide to achieving financial independence, tailored to diverse groups such as young adults, single parents, freelancers, retirees, and minorities. Here, we summarize the key principles discussed throughout the book to reinforce the main points and provide a clear roadmap for readers.

Understanding Your Financial Situation

Assess Current Finances: Evaluate your income, expenses, debts, and assets to get a clear picture of your financial health.

Create a Personal Balance Sheet: List all assets and liabilities to understand your net worth.

Set a Baseline: Establish your starting point to measure progress over time.

Track Progress: Continuously monitor your finances to stay on track with your goals.

Setting Clear Financial Goals

Importance of Goals: Setting financial goals provides direction and motivation.

SMART Goals: Ensure your goals are Specific, Measurable, Achievable, Relevant, and Time-bound for effective planning and tracking.

Budgeting Basics

Creating a Budget: Develop a budget that outlines your income and expenses, ensuring you allocate funds effectively.

Tracking Expenses: Use methods like apps or spreadsheets to monitor daily, weekly, and monthly spending.

Adjusting Your Budget: Regularly review and tweak your budget to accommodate changes in income or expenses.

Saving Strategies for Everyone

Building an Emergency Fund: Establish a safety net to cover unexpected expenses.

Automatic Savings: Set up automatic transfers to savings accounts to ensure consistent saving.

Finding Extra Savings: Identify areas to cut expenses and save more, such as reducing discretionary spending.

Managing Debt

Types of Debt: Understand the difference between good and bad debt.

Debt Repayment Strategies: Utilize methods like the debt snowball or avalanche to pay off debts efficiently.

Avoiding Debt Traps: Stay out of unnecessary debt by living within your means and avoiding high-interest loans.

Income Enhancement

Multiple Income Streams: Diversify income sources to reduce financial risk and increase earnings.

Side Hustles: Explore side hustles that align with your skills and interests.

Maximizing Earnings: Use negotiation tactics to secure higher salaries or rates.

Basics of Investing

Why Invest?: Investing is crucial for long-term wealth growth and financial security.

Types of Investments: Understand the various investment options like stocks, bonds, real estate, mutual funds, and ETFs.

Starting Small: Begin investing with limited funds, focusing on low-cost, diversified options.

Long-Term Financial Planning

Retirement Planning: Start planning for retirement early to ensure a comfortable future.

Retirement Accounts: Familiarize yourself with retirement accounts such as 401(k)s, IRAs, and options available in different countries like India's NPS and PPF.

Legacy Planning: Plan your estate to ensure your financial legacy is secure and your wishes are honored.

Financial Strategies for Specific Groups

Young Adults: Focus on managing student loans, building credit, and starting to invest early.

Single Parents: Budget on a single income, seek financial aid, and plan for children's futures.

Freelancers and Gig Workers: Manage irregular income, save for taxes, and invest in retirement.

Retirees or Near-Retirees: Maximize retirement income, manage healthcare costs, and plan your legacy.

Minorities and Underrepresented Groups: Overcome financial barriers, access resources, and build community wealth.

Tools and Resources

Financial Tools: Use apps and software for budgeting, investing, and tracking finances.

Books and Websites: Continue your financial education with recommended reading and reliable online resources.

Community Support: Build a support network and find financial mentors to guide you on your journey.

Real-Life Success Stories

Case Studies: Learn from inspirational stories of individuals who achieved financial independence.

Lessons Learned: Apply practical advice and strategies from real-life examples to your own situation.

Conclusion

Achieving financial independence is a journey that requires careful planning, disciplined execution, and continuous learning. By understanding your financial situation, setting clear goals, budgeting wisely, managing debt, enhancing income, investing smartly, planning for the long term, and leveraging available resources and community support, you can take control of your financial future. The real-life success stories and lessons learned demonstrate that financial independence is attainable for everyone, regardless of background or starting point. Stay committed to your goals, remain adaptable, and keep educating yourself to navigate the complexities of personal finance successfully.

Next Steps

Achieving financial independence is a journey that starts with small, actionable steps. Here are simple steps readers can take immediately to begin their path toward financial independence:

1. Assess Your Financial Situation

Gather Financial Documents: Collect all relevant financial documents, including bank statements, bills, loan information, and investment records.

Create a Personal Balance Sheet: List all your assets (cash, investments, property) and liabilities (debts, loans) to determine your net worth.

Track Your Spending: Use a notebook, spreadsheet, or budgeting app to record your daily expenses for at least a month. This will help you understand where your money is going.

2. Set Clear Financial Goals

Define Your Goals: Identify short-term (within 1 year), medium-term (1-5 years), and long-term (5+ years) financial goals. Be specific about what you want to achieve.

Prioritize: Rank your goals by importance and urgency. Focus on one or two major goals at a time to avoid feeling overwhelmed.

3. Create a Budget

Draft a Monthly Budget: Allocate your income to cover essential expenses (housing, food, utilities), debt repayments, savings, and discretionary spending.

Use the 50/30/20 Rule: As a guideline, aim to spend 50% of your income on needs, 30% on wants, and allocate 20% for savings and debt repayment.

4. Start Saving

Build an Emergency Fund: Aim to save at least $1,000 initially, then work towards having 3-6 months' worth of living expenses in a readily accessible savings account.

Automate Your Savings: Set up automatic transfers from your checking account to your savings account to ensure you save consistently.

5. Manage Your Debt

List Your Debts: Write down all your debts, including interest rates, minimum payments, and due dates.

Choose a Repayment Strategy: Decide whether to use the snowball method (paying off the smallest debts first) or the avalanche method (paying off the highest interest debts first).

6. Enhance Your Income

Explore Side Hustles: Identify opportunities to earn extra income based on your skills and interests, such as freelancing, tutoring, or selling handmade goods.

Improve Your Skills: Invest in education or training to enhance your qualifications and increase your earning potential.

7. Begin Investing

Start Small: Open an investment account with a small initial amount. Consider low-cost index funds or ETFs to diversify your investments.

Learn the Basics: Educate yourself about different types of investments and risk management strategies. Online courses, books, and financial blogs can be useful resources.

8. Plan for the Long Term

Retirement Planning: If you haven't already, open a retirement account (such as a 401(k), IRA, or equivalent in your country) and start contributing regularly.

Set Up Automatic Contributions: Ensure a portion of your income goes directly into your retirement account each month.

9. Seek Support and Resources

Use Financial Tools: Leverage budgeting apps, investment platforms, and financial calculators to manage your finances efficiently.

Join a Community: Engage with financial literacy groups, online forums, or local workshops to build a support network and gain insights from others.

10. Stay Informed and Adapt

Continuous Education: Commit to ongoing learning about personal finance. Read books, follow financial blogs, and listen to podcasts to stay updated.

Review and Adjust: Regularly review your financial goals and strategies. Adjust your plans as needed based on changes in your financial situation or goals.

By taking these steps, you can build a solid foundation for your journey towards financial independence. Remember, the key is to start small, stay consistent, and continuously adapt to your changing circumstances. Every step you take brings you closer to achieving financial stability and independence.